MENU
·design
5

MENU
design
5

by

Judi Radice
with the

NATIONAL
RESTAURANT
ASSOCIATION

Library of Applied Design

An Imprint of

PBC INTERNATIONAL, INC. ✦ NEW YORK

Distributor to the book trade in the United States and Canada:

Rizzoli International Publications Inc.
300 Park Avenue South
New York, NY 10010

Distributor to the art trade in the United States and Canada:

PBC International, Inc.
One School Street
Glen Cove, NY 11542
1-800-527-2826
Fax 516-676-2738

Distributor throughout the rest of the world:

Hearst Books International
1350 Avenue of the Americas
New York, NY 10019

Library of Congress Cataloging-in-Publication Data

Radice, Judi
    Menu design 5: marketing the restaurant through graphics / by
Judi Radice.
        p.   cm.
    Includes index.
    ISBN 0-86636-180-4
    1. Menu design.   I. Title   II. Title: Menu design five.
NC1002.M4R34   1992
647.95'068'8--dc20
                                                92-16750
                                                     CIP

CAVEAT—Information in this text is believed accurate, and will pose no
problem for the student or casual reader. However, the author was often
constrained by information contained in signed release forms, information
that could have been in error or not included at all. Any misinformation (or
lack of information) is the result of failure in these attestations. The author
has done whatever is possible to insure accuracy.

Printed in Hong Kong

Typography by
Jeanne Weinberg Typesetting

10 9 8 7 6 5 4 3 2 1

To Michael Hughes...
you have inspired me to realize my dreams
and I am forever grateful.

Acknowledgments

With help from some very talented people, this book has become a reality. Most importantly, I would like to acknowledge all the great design represented in this project. It is a combination of restaurateurs with vision and designers with the ability to carry out that vision that make the entries in this book a valuable resource.

I would like to say a special thanks to those people who devoted their energies to this project, particularly Victoria Rabiner for coordinating the call-for-entries. I would also like to thank Marti Moore for assisting me with the organization and research of the book and for helping make the project go so smoothly. Christian Simon, an intern from San Jose State University, with a keen proofing eye, assisted me in verying the text. I am grateful to the following people who interviewed, Bruce Yelaska for his design expertise and to Rod Dyer for his perspective as a designer and a restaurateur. I owe a debt of gratitude to Marcy Lansing of Levy Restaurants in Chicago and to David Carter of David Carter Design in Dallas for their interviews and points of view. I would like to give a special thanks to my parents who continue to collect menus for me and to all my dear friends, colleagues and clients who continued to be supportive of me and my work.

Eight years ago I never dreamed I would be producing the fifth in this series of books on menu design. On that note, I would like to thank my friends at PBC International whose commitment to producing quality books continues. I would like to make special mention of Kevin Clark who has encouraged me beyond my potential. And thanks too to Carrie Abel for her jacket design, Laurie Coskiano for successfully promoting my books, Chet Dallas for rewriting and editing the text, and to Penny, Mark, Joanne, Bedelia and Gary.

Most of all, I want to thank the readers of this book who continue to inspire me to seek out the best possible examples in menu design.

Judi Radice
San Francisco, 1992

Table of Contents

Chapter 1   14
Down Under

Menus with a seafood theme are featured in this chapter where flexibility is the key criteria.

Chapter 2   26
The Good Earth

Whether it be in the restaurant's concept, or the material chosen to produce the menu, or the graphics used, these menus are all based upon themes of earth and nature.

Chapter 3   38
Now That's Italian!

With the popularity of restaurants featuring the regional cuisines of Italy, comes an array of design solutions. This chapter demonstrates the variety of offerings in food, culture, and design for Italian restaurants.

Chapter 4   60
Americana

This chapter is represented by tradition, nostalgia, old engravings, eclectic photographs, and collages that are used to create images evocative of American life past and present.

Chapter 5   70
Unique Materials

Menu durability is one of the main concerns for many restaurateurs, but at the same time there is a need for the flexibility to make pricing and selection changes. In this chapter everything from corkboard, chipboard, aluminum and even Hawaiian koa wood has been used to devise unique menu designs.

Chapter 6   92
Ethnic Menus

Whether a French bistro, Greek taverna, a Southwestern theme or Native American ambience, these menus take on the characteristics indicative of the region or culture they represent.

Chapter 7   108
By Air, by Land, by Sea

Beyond restaurants, menus are used in many different phases of our everyday lives. This chapter represents some of the unusual places menus turn up including commercial airlines, passenger trains, hospitals, universities and cruise ships.

FOREWORD

Adversity is the mother of invention—and often great menu design, too.

For 10 consecutive years ending in 1989, the restaurant industry experienced steady growth. People felt confident about the future. They had money. They wanted amusement, and they regarded restaurants as entertainment. So they ate out.

Then came adversity. Actually, customers began to retrench in the late '80s, but we date the big change from July, 1990, when the consumer confidence index fell 17 points and then continued to fall through January for a total of 47 points. When people lose confidence in their economic future, they try to cut their expenditure. In fact, during this recession people did not stop eating out, but they did limit their spending. Either they chose a less expensive restaurant, or they ordered less in their usual haunts.

How did restaurateurs respond? At the lower end, they offered specials, deals, coupons—anything to bring the price down and customer counts up. At the upper end, the response was more penetrating. Recession meant a change of culture. The elegant, exotic, exclusive was out; the homey, familiar and casual was in. Casualization meant creating simpler menu items from less expensive ingredients, and that, in turn, meant lower prices.

Of course, menu design changed, too. As one judge of our Great Menu Contest commented, "Never have I seen so many single-panel menus from restaurants that used to hand out vellum bound in leather." He was referring to the single laminated panel with art and name on one side and food listings on the other. These menus are less expensive; many are striking, and they manage to set the new casual tone.

Certainly, there has been a trend toward casual and less costly menus. This year, we have seen effective menus printed in one color, sharp menus based on wit and clip art, and prize-winning menus designed around artwork by customers. But, at the same time, we have seen a counter-trend. This book contains a significant number of beautifully designed menus produced from costly materials.

You see, most restaurateurs believe that when customer counts fall, it is time to spend money on marketing and promotion. And the menu is the restaurateur's primary marketing tool. Recession or not, this past year's Great Menu Contest winners included the stunning menu from Edwardo's (page 48) and the beautiful, die-cut catering menu from the Hyatt Regency (Page 172), to name just two casual menus that were by no means inexpensive.

As we go to press, the economists seem to agree that the recession is ending. Certainly, we are feeling a new stirring in our business. Still, a return to the extravagance of the '80s seems unlikely. Tastes have changed, and the casual mood will prevail. If I had to select one menu that typifies what we are seeing in foodservice today, I would point to the menu from the Blue Mesa Grill (page 95), which is striking, simple and user-friendly.

John R. Farquharson
President and
Chairman of the Board
National Restaurant Association

Introduction

In today's competitive restaurant market, with its cost conscious value-attuned consumers, restaurants must provide excellent food at a good value whatever the price range. But good value isn't the only priority. An increasingly sophisticated clientele is looking for a complete dining experience, demanding entertainment as well as imagination when eating out. Successful restaurants have learned that they must maximize customer satisfaction while working within the confines of cost restrictions.

A major player in a restaurant's personality is the menu. No other single factor affords a better opportunity for portrayal of the restaurant's character. A menu, beside serving as a guide for food and beverage selection, can enrich and complement its design philosophy.

Menu Design 5 showcases outstanding examples that provide a strong personality for their restaurants, from the patriotic pop-up for the Grand Hotel on Mackinac Island, Michigan; to the cork-faced menu featured at Grand Street Cafe in San Francisco; to the oversized (14"x20") flexible menus featured at Galeto's in New York City. These menus successfully portray the "heart and soul" of their respective establishments. They visually alert the customer to the restaurant's food offerings and ambience. In other words—they tell a story.

CHAPTER

1

Down
Under

The folder style menus were created to reinforce the rich colors apparent in the space. The interior pages of the menus are of gray simulated parchment that correspond to the restaurant's gray marble. The restaurant resembles a neoclassical piazza, with dark ceilings that evoke a night sky. The walls are ochre and the floor a blue-green stone. There is a subtle 3-D seascape that spans the length of the marble bar. The exhibition style kitchen is the focal point of the restaurant with all the tables arranged in a gentle semi-circle around it.

Tutto Mare

RESTAURANT/OPERATOR
Tutto Mare Ristorante/
Spectrum Foods, Inc.
San Diego, CA
YEAR OPENED
1991
DESIGN FIRM
Primo Angeli, Inc.
ART DIRECTOR
Lisa Sanford
PRINTER
Mastercraft

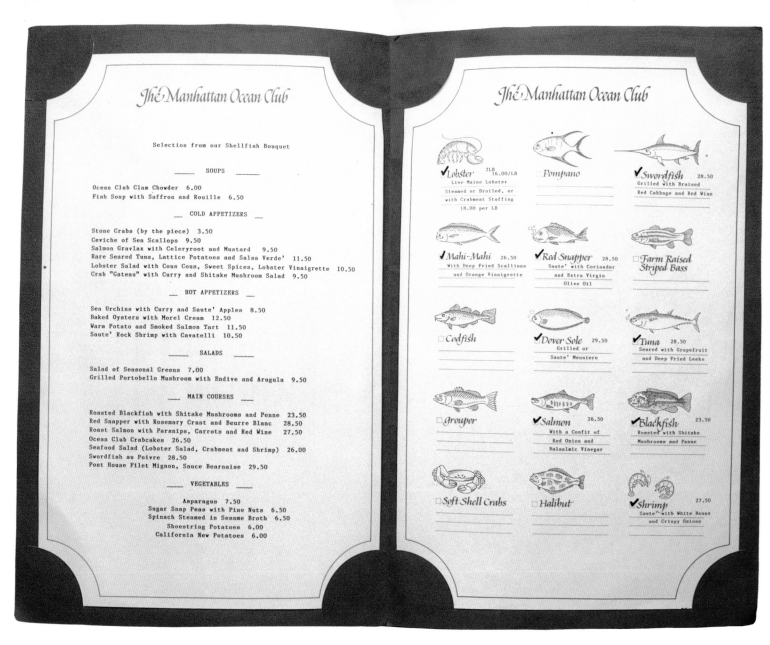

The Manhattan Ocean Club

RESTAURANT/OPERATOR
The Manhattan Ocean Club
The New York Restaurant Group
New York, NY
YEAR OPENED
1983
DESIGN FIRM
Rossin Studios
DESIGNER
Linda Rossin

The Manhattan Ocean Club's goal was to have a menu design which would allow fish selections to change daily in order to serve the freshest available choices. What makes this oversize menu so exciting is its illustrated chart. The versatile sheets are cleverly designed so the chef can actually check off what is available and write in a description and price for each day. This format makes it fun for customers.

Lobster & Champagne

RESTAURANT/OPERATOR
The Grange/Adelaide Hilton
Adelaide, Australia
YEAR OPENED
1982
DESIGN FIRM
In house design
DESIGNER
A. Sapio
PRINTER
APS Printers

The Hilton Hotel created this lobster
and champagne menu to celebrate the
lobster season. The menu design
needed to be upscale and formal since
it represents one of the Hilton Hotel's
premier restaurants. The menu cover
contains a die-cut ampersand revealing
a handmade paper affixed from
behind; this technique gives a sense of
depth and texture.

La Rive Summer

RESTAURANT/OPERATOR
La Rive/Oyster Point Hotel
YEAR OPENED
1978
DESIGN FIRM
The Menu Design Group, Inc.
DESIGNER
W. Scott Mahr
ILLUSTRATOR
Liz Kearney
PRINTER
B.C. Lucas

La Rive wanted a seafood menu that
honored the elegance of the location
without relying on the typical fare of
whaler memorabilia and fishnets. The
designer's challenge was to create the
image of an elegant and trendy seafood
house. The menu's subtle design with
die-cut pages and an airbrushed
illustration has a loose, fluid look
evocative of the sea.

The Third Floor Fish Cafe

RESTAURANT/OPERATOR
**The Third Floor Fish Cafe/
LLC Restaurants
Kirkland, WA**
DESIGN FIRM
The Menu Workshop
DESIGNER
Margo Christianson
ART DIRECTOR
Liz Kearney
ILLUSTRATOR
Margo Christianson
PRINTER
Espresso Press

Associate Art Director Margo Christianson says, "the fun thing about this project was that it was a successful makeover of a steak house. The interior has a lot of dark wood inside and the restaurant tended to feel sort of stuffy. The client needed help to make the transition to a lighter, more upbeat seafood spot." An important feature of this program was to add flexibility. Menu changes can be made daily by imprinting an existing master sheet with an in-house laser printer. Most importantly, the design concept is kept intact. "The results have been outstanding," states Christianson, "with a 35 percent increase in sales since this new concept and menu package were put into place. The work included logo development for lunch, dinner, bar, children's and dessert menus. There are table tents, basket liners for items like fish and chips, as well as signage in support of the menu design."

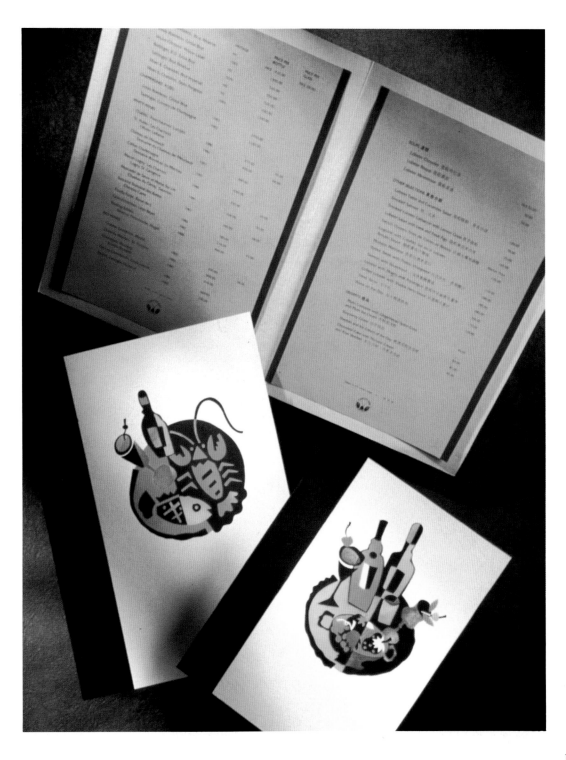

Lobster Bar

RESTAURANT/OPERATOR
Lobster Bar/Island Shangri-la
Hong Kong
YEAR OPENED
1991
DESIGN FIRM
David Carter Graphic Design
DESIGNER
Waitak Lai

The Lobster Bar is a lighthearted casual seafood restaurant located in the Island Shangri-la Hong Kong Hotel. At the center of the restaurant is the primary attraction—a tank full of live lobsters. The lunch menu consists of fresh lobster selections and a drinks menu printed in two languages. The contemporary stylized illustrations and lobster motif tie the theme together.

The Smith Brothers Fish Shanty

RESTAURANT/OPERATOR
**The Smith Brothers Fish Shanty/
De Rosa Corporation
Wauwatosa, WI**
YEAR OPENED
1934
DESIGN FIRM
**Miller Meester Advertising and
Z Studio Design & Illustration**
DESIGNER
Matt Zumbo
ART DIRECTOR
Doug Engel
ILLUSTRATOR
Matt Zumbo
PRINTER
Sells Printing

APPETIZERS

Onion Strings
Homemade in our own kitchen, try this mountain of crunchy onion taste with a frosty cold draft from the bar. Yes sir, you got the right one baby. **2.65**

Deep Dish Pizza Soup
Sweet Italian sausage, onions, garlic, mushrooms, tomatoes and spices all blended in a tomato based broth that's smothered with fresh mozzarella cheese and seasoned croutons. A Smith Brothers original. **2.95**

Almond Catfish Bites
Excuse me, could this be paradise? Light, flaky catfish hand-breaded in our own homemade almond crunch. Send the kids home early, you might want a double-order. **4.65**

Tortilla Crunchies
First check your pulse because these are gonna set your mouth to dancin'. Then ask your server to place this order of seven stuffed golden brown tortillas where no one else can get at 'em. Shot on goal. It's good! **4.65**

The Mozzarella Stomp
Shake your hips. Groove your move. And bite into five of the chewiest Wisconsin mozzarella cheese fingers served alongside a marinara sauce so tangy, you'll smile. **3.25**

Cream Cheese & Crab Wontons
Wimpy thinks he could live on these alone. A delectable mix of cream cheese and crabmeat stuffed within a lightly fried wonton skin. Man your battlestations, there's gonna be a war over these. **3.95**

Chicken Crunch
Don't blink, everyone grabs for these hand-breaded strips of lightly seasoned chicken so quickly, it's looks like the end of Sunday mass in a resort town. Served with honey mustard or sweet and sour. **4.25**

German Wontons
Lawdy mama, what have we here? It tastes like the best Reuben you've every had, but it looks like it just got off the boat from China. Kind of an East meets West, Vern. **2.95**

Slow Potato Boats
Smothered with melted cream cheese, green onion, seafood and crab, these potato boats will set your mind adrift to the imaginary island of Kenosha, somewhere off the coast of Racine. (Now would be the time to say a prayer for the menu writer's quick recovery, folks.) **4.95**

Calamari Crunch
Park the Hudson, Mom, this one says we're home. Hand-breaded in our kitchen, lightly seasoned, and served with a dipping sauce so tangy, it begs you think about ordering 12 ounces of what made Milwaukee famous. **4.45**

Smitty's Sampler For Two
Onion strings, mozzarella fingers, tortilla crunchies and the kitchen sink. We started this one so you might realize inner peace as to the wisdom of your solution to the great appetizer dilemma—what the hell I'm gonna have here? **5.95**

Shrimp Cocktail
Not an ordinary shrimp cocktail, an extraordinary shrimp cocktail with fresh shrimp so tasty, you'll think you're sitting gulfside feeling the ocean breeze. **5.25**

Homemade Clam Chowder
This one's got so many chunks of potato and clams in it, you hear the cook moaning to the strains of *Oh, Danny Boy*, nursing a bottle of Bushmill's. **2.45**

Neptune Fish Chowder
A tomato based chowder chock-full of fish, celery, carrots and mushrooms. A great meal in itself. **2.45**

BOAT RULES

1. If the fishin' is real good, our doors may be closed.

2. It's every customer's sworn right to lie about the size of the last fish they caught. But ours was still bigger.

3. If your dinner is not to your liking, we'll start over.

4. Our goal is hot food hot, cold food cold.

5. Anyone caught behaving like a yuppie will be asked to leave.

6. We always serve the freshest fish possible.

7. We treat all our customers the same — lousy, but at least we don't play favorites.

8. Spend it all, we've never seen an armored car in a funeral.

9. There's more to life than money and getting ahead, so please check your worries at the door.

10. Saying grace before dinner is not only okay, it's encouraged.

11. From time to time, you may see a bartender in the dining room, please don't feed 'em.

12. As much as you love our fish, we ask that you not date them.

13. If something's wrong, please speak up, it's the only way we can learn from our mistakes.

14. If you go away hungry, we starve.

15. We believe in the Cubs, a longer St. Patrick's Day, equal rights for all, that we are the children our parents warned us about, Travis McGee, the power of laughter, drive-in movies, romance, that we're doin' it all for our kids, and finally, helping others. So, if the spirit moves you, make a little donation to the MS Society. —Thanks.

"YOUR HONOR, THE DEFENDANT _SWEARS_ HE NEVER SERVED A FISH IN HIS LIFE."

G. PETERS

Overlooking Lake Michigan in Port Washington, Wisconsin, The Smith Brothers Fish Shanty certainly lives up to its name. The design intent of their menu was to casualize the restaurant from a formal dinner house to one with a more fun and lively atmosphere. The initial redesign with a brown kraft cover was the first in an evolution of menu designs. The second progression was a white menu cover that shifted the focus from a seafood oriented one to a more playful theme with seafood as its primary selection. This was accomplished by using lively graphics, bright colors and clever writing. The various sections are easy to read because of their distinctive typographic design.

This menu won a Second Prize in the NRA's 1991 awards in the "Average Check Over $15" category.

Big City Fish

RESTAURANT/OPERATOR
Big City Fish/Big City Fish
Joint Venture
Coconut Grove, FL
YEAR OPENED
1991
DESIGN FIRM
Patrick McBride Company
DESIGNER
Raymond Kampf
ILLUSTRATOR
Raymond Kampf

Big City Fish has its roots in hearty portions in an environment with an industrial look. The goal was to give the guest a menu that "meant business" and yet was not cumbersome. The client also needed the ability to update the fresh fish at a moment's notice.

The interior of Big City Fish grew out of the idea to recreate the atmosphere of a waterside fish plant. The designer was searching for an urban, industrial warehouse look as opposed to the more commonly found "Cannery Row motif." The logo played a major part in establishing the look of the family of graphics. References to food company logos of the '30s and '40s served as a design inspiration. The '50s truck stop placemats and a 150-foot mural blend to create a highly aggressive environment. The mural, depicting the interior of a fish processing plant, was inspired by the WPA. The "fun element" shows a subtle, sophisticated and stylized sense of humor.

The construction of the menu consists of acetate pockets glued to the interior panels of the aluminum cover. The pockets hold a slip-in laser printed sheet.

f i s h

These items represent the freshest product available today. We have listed the chefs recommended preparation and sauce with each item, however, feel free to ask your server to have it prepared the way you want and with any one of the listed sauces

PREPARATION	FISH	SAUCE	
grilled	wahoo	lime beurre	
		blanc	9.35
blackened	dolphin		9.85
broiled	black grouper	creole	8.65
hot smoked	mackerel	dill mayonnaise	6.30
grilled	tuna	soy ginger	10.75

b.b.q. belt served with cole slaw and baked beans

pork ribs – "st. louis" smoked and grilled	1lb -11.25	2lbs -18.75	
bbq chicken – smoked and grilled			6.45
mixed bbq plate – ribs, chicken and smoked sausage			12.15
cowboy steak– grilled 28oz. bone-in rib cut			21.85

specialities

shrimp creole – sauteed shrimp, peppers, onions, celery and tomato with rice	8.85
fried shrimp and/or oyster platter – with hush puppies, french fries,	
tartar and cocktail sauce	9.25
grilled smoked swordfish – served with red horseradish sauce and	
big city vegetables	12.90
whole baked stuffed flounder – crab meat stuffing	14.85
panfried snapper – tempura batter, in a soy ginger glaze, served	
with big city vegetables	9.65
soft shell crab – fried, in a cilantro brown butter served	
with big city vegetables	11.85
crab meat au gratin – fresh lump crabmeat baked with cheese mornay sauce	10.85
grilled salmon – served with tomato and garlic hollandaise sauce	
and big city vegetables	12.15
florida stone crab claws – served with woody's mustard sauce–1 lb.	19.95
fried seafood platter – shrimp, oysters, fresh fish, stuffed crab,	
crab claws, hush puppies and tartar sauce	16.85

sandwiches & po-boys served with french fries

shrimp po-boy –fried with shredded lettuce, tartar sauce,	
ketchup and tomato on french bread	7.75
oyster po-boy –fried with shredded lettuce, tartar sauce,	
ketchup and tomato on french bread	6.75
bbq beef – on a kaiser roll	5.50
hamburger – half pound on a kaiser roll	5.75
chicken breast sandwich – grilled, on a kaiser roll with hoisin bbq sauce	5.75
fish sandwich – daily catch on a kaiser roll–ask your server	6.95

● big city fish has facilities for private parties
call 445-CITY (2489) for inquiries

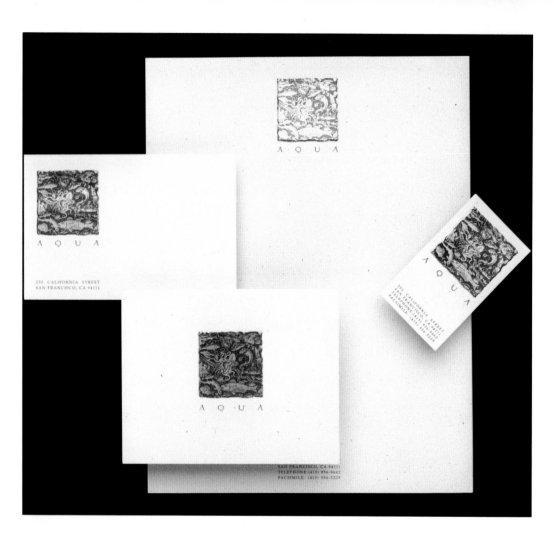

Aqua

RESTAURANT/OPERATOR
Aqua
San Francisco, CA
YEAR OPENED
1991
DESIGN FIRM
Anthony C. Eglin Advertising/
Frost Tsuji
DESIGNER
Tony Eglin
ART DIRECTOR
Wendy Tsuji
ILLUSTRATOR
Wade Hoefer
PRINTER
Reliable Graphics, Inc.

This collaboration between the design firm and the architects on the project, Frost Tsuji, resulted in an inspired menu design. The typical menu with the restaurant logo would not do for this upscale seafood house, as they wanted a menu that reflected as closely as possible the recurring theme of artist Wade Hoefer's paintings that hang in the restaurant. It also reinforces the restaurant's sophisticated, yet unpretentious theme via a series of three varying menu covers.

Water Grill

RESTAURANT/OPERATOR
Water Grill
University Restaurant Group
Los Angeles, CA
YEAR OPENED
1991
DESIGN FIRM
Mary Oeffling Design
DESIGNER
Mary Oeffling
ART DIRECTOR
Merrill Gilbert-Harrell
ILLUSTRATOR
Ann Field
PRINTER
Castle Press

The fossil-like surfaces, fish lamps and other sea-inspired lighting, subtle water pattern upholstery and colors, all work to enhance the Water Grill's theme. A mural illustrated by artist Ann Field, of playful sea life and local Los Angeles landmarks, adorns the interior walls. These images are reproduced on the menu cover to reflect the light mood evident in the restaurant's decor, while counterbalancing the quality of the restaurant's food and service. The design was based on a need to accommodate a daily printed menu and highlight the oyster bar, the centerpiece of the restaurant. The entree pages introduce seafood from all regions of the United States and consist of food and wines that complement these selections.

CHAPTER

2

The
Good
Earth

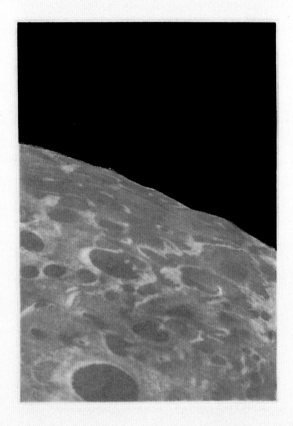

NEW YEAR'S EVE 1 9 9 0

Orange and bitter almond apéritif

Shellfish cocktail

Oysters fried in potato nests, caviar cream

Raviolini of celery root in black truffle bouillon

Crown roast of Lewis Ranch lamb with chestnuts

Ragoût of boletes, horns of plenty, and chanterelles

Brandied raspberry soufflé crêpe $100.

BLUE MOON · CHEZ PANISSE

Chez Panisse New Year's Eve 1990

RESTAURANT/OPERATOR
Chez Panisse
Berkeley, CA
DESIGN FIRM
Patricia Curtan Design & Printing
DESIGNER
Patricia Curtan
ILLUSTRATORS
Patricia Curtan & Stephen Thomas

As the saying goes, a blue moon comes out but once in a while. This presented an opportunity for a clever menu theme for New Year's Eve 1990 dinner at Chez Panisse. The Berkeley restaurant that first brought us California cuisine, celebrated this special occasion with a limited edition of handmade menus. These exquisite mementos, produced with special care by designer Patricia Curtan, were done on her letterpress.

The Oak Tree

RESTAURANT/OPERATOR
The Oak Tree
Chicago, IL
YEAR OPENED
1991 (new location)
DESIGN FIRM
Printed Concepts, Inc.
DESIGNER
Scott Hanselman
ART DIRECTOR
Carmen Maugeri
ILLUSTRATOR
Michael DeJong
PRINTER
Rohner Printing (6 color labels),
Riverside Graphics (2 color body)

The original Oak Tree is a landmark in Chicago's Gold Coast neighborhood. Last year, their original location was demolished and the restaurant relocated to the prestigious 900 North Michigan Avenue, a multi-level mall that houses Bloomingdale's Department Store. This change of location required a new image that would be flexible and accommodate the trimmed hours of operation and a slightly different clientele.

The menu itself became a critical starting point establishing a framework for the rest of the project. The designer created a connected, compartmentalized style for each of the meal periods. Michael DeJong, an established New York painter, was commissioned to create three paintings illustrating the changing cycle in the restaurant's day. The paintings enhance the interior's whimsical garden theme. As customers enter The Oak Tree they are greeted by flower boxes filled with fresh daisies and ivy. To start the day on a bright note, the daisies appear on the oversized breakfast menu. Illustrated poppies make the lunch menu inviting and complement a red floral mural painted on the restaurant's east wall. A detailed illustration of a grape cluster is found on the dinner and specials menu, and on the wine card. These graphics echo the painting that represents the evening cycle.

The menu's front cover is an earthy, yet economical sheet of recycled stock from packing paper suppliers. The sheet is dry mounted on recycled commercial cover weight stock, and embossed and scored to accommodate the label illustrations.

28

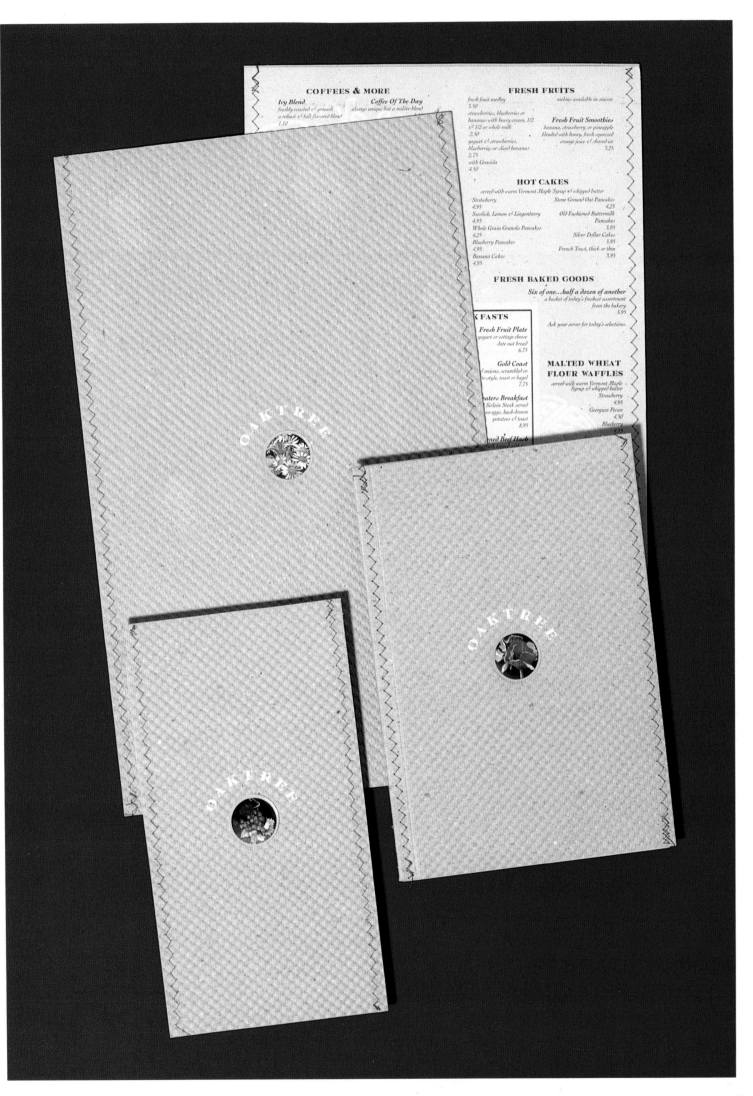

Island Cafe

RESTAURANT/OPERATOR
**Island Cafe/Island Shangri-la,
Hong Kong**
YEAR OPENED
1990
DESIGN FIRM
David Carter Graphic Design
DESIGNER
Lori Wilson
ILLUSTRATOR
Waitak Lai
PRINTER
Goodwill Printing

The Island Cafe, a California-style restaurant in Hong Kong that serves fresh, light cuisine wanted a menu that would convey just such a look. Peach trees dominate the decor lending a distinctive design element. To further enhance this theme, the logo duplicates a stamp one might find on a crate used to ship fresh fruit. Each menu cover features a surprinted logo of fruits grown in California. Freestyle calligraphy wraps around the illustrations describing the taste and texture of each fruit. A miniature fruit crate filled with crayons is placed on each table for the entertainment of younger guests.

The flowers used on the menus were designed to incorporate the floral atmosphere of the restaurant's oriental garden decor with subtle Chinese detailing. Katherine Truitt, a floral designer, was hired to press the flowers to match those found in the restaurant. The designer incorporated a unique raffia tie to create a more custom look to the overall design.

Canton Garden

RESTAURANT/OPERATOR
Canton Garden
Grand Hyatt Taipei
Taipei Taiwan R.O.C.
YEAR OPENED
1990
DESIGN FIRM
David Carter Graphic Design
DESIGNER
Lori Wilson
ILLUSTRATOR
Pressed Flowers by Katherine Truitt
PRINTER
Jarvis Press

Cuisine Naturelle

RESTAURANT/OPERATOR
Hyatt Hotels & Resorts
Chicago, IL
DESIGN FIRM
Associates
DESIGNER
Donna Milord
PHOTOGRAPHER
stock photography
PRINTER
Associates

Hyatt Hotels and Resorts recognizes that today's traveler is looking for a light and healthy meal and have in turn developed a light spa-style cuisine. Their contribution was to develop this menu with its photograph of a prairie panorama. Produced as a blank shell it is individualized for each operation throughout the chain.

Coffee Tree

RESTAURANT/OPERATOR
Nut Tree
Nut Tree, CA
YEAR OPENED
1965 (Coffee Tree)
DESIGN FIRM
Nut Tree Design
DESIGNER
Daniel Salcedo
ART DIRECTOR
Michael Green
ILLUSTRATOR
Ruth Dicker
PRINTER
Ulatis Creek

As an extension of the Nut Tree operation, the Coffee Tree restaurant was established in March of 1965. Their current menu captures the essence of Solano County, California with its lavish illustrations of wildflowers, golden hills, orchards, and of course the famous springtime California poppies. The illustrations are inspired by photographs of elements from the main decorative relief panels of painted wood. Simple and clean layout design make this menu a delight.

Fruits & Juices

Apple Juice 1.55
Freshly Squeezed Orange Juice or Grapefruit Juice 1.95
Tomato Juice 1.50
Western Fruit Bowl 5.75
Fresh Pineapple Spears 2.95
Half Grapefruit 2.75
Bananas & Cream 2.35
Melons in Season 2.95
Yogurt & Fruit 3.95
A generous bowl of yogurt, topped with seasonal fruit.

Breakfasts

Two Eggs 3.95
& Bacon 5.95
& Sausage 5.95
& Ham 5.95
& Canadian Style Bacon 6.50
& Steak 8.95
Above served with either potatoes and toast, or with pancakes.

Coffee Tree Pizza Style Omelet 6.95
With your choice of Ham, Bacon or Sausage 7.95
An open-faced three-egg omelet sprinkled with grated cheese, fresh mushrooms and cherry tomato halves.

Huevos Rancheros 7.25
A crisp or soft tortilla topped with black bean chili, Mexican sauce, two eggs, and bacon strips. Served with chayote salsa.

Stuffed French Toast 6.50
A Nut Tree loaf of bread filled with thin slices of ham, Swiss cheese, and our own pineapple and cherry jam, dipped into an egg batter and grilled golden brown.

Waffle 3.95
Dollar Sized Pancakes 4.50
Pancakes 4.50
Short Stack Pancakes 3.95
Blueberry Pancakes 4.50
Short Stack Blueberry Pancakes 3.95
French Toast 4.50

Pastries

Danish Pastry 2.50
Croissants 2.50
Regular or honey wheat.
Coffee Cake for Two 3.25
Blueberry, Orange-Nut or Date-Nut served warm with butter.
Half Coffee Cake 2.25
Apple Log or
Apricot Log 1.95
Muffins 1.95
Pumpkin, blueberry or apple.
Nut Roll 1.95
Crumpet 1.95

Garden Court Bistro

RESTAURANT/OPERATOR
Garden Court Bistro
ITT Sheraton Hotel
Anaheim, CA
YEAR OPENED
1991
DESIGN FIRM
On The Edge
DESIGNER
Jeff Gasper
ART DIRECTOR
Joe Mozdzen
ILLUSTRATOR
Jeff Gasper
PRINTER
Sand Graphics
PAPER
Parchment

The new logo and menu design for the recently remodeled Garden Court Bistro located in the Sheraton Anaheim Hotel, reflects a soft Mediterranean palette. Parchment-like marbleized paper, in conjunction with patina green and weathered gold inks, harkens back to the Renaissance, while complementing the natural imagery of the food. With curable clear plastic jackets, this menu shows its versatility by complementing the elegance of fine dining while serving the needs of a high-volume hotel restaurant.

33

Bakeries By The Bay

RESTAURANT/OPERATOR
Bakeries By The Bay
San Francisco, CA
YEAR OPENED
1991
DESIGN FIRM
Tharp Did It
DESIGNER
Jean Mogannam
ART DIRECTOR
Rick Tharp
PRINTER
Forman/Leibrock

The Bakeries By The Bay logo was
developed as a corporate symbol for a
chain of retail bakeries in San
Francisco. It represents the sun rising
over the San Francisco Bay and
reminds us of freshly baked goods in
the morning. The sun's rays are
comprised of thirteen wheat shafts,
symbolizing a baker's dozen, the
generous bakers' tradition of adding a
little something extra for good luck.

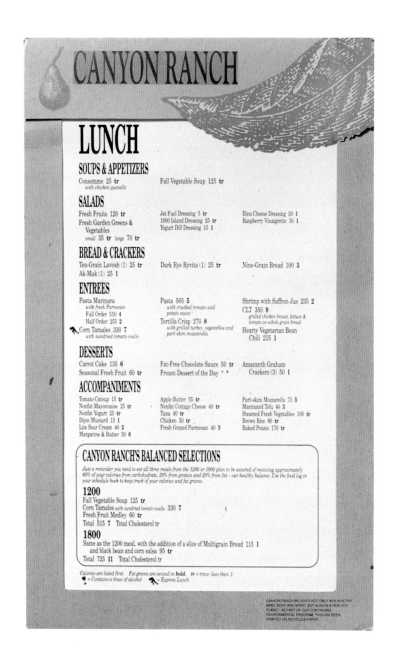

Canyon Ranch Spas

RESTAURANT/OPERATOR
Canyon Ranch
Tucson, AZ
DESIGN FIRM
The Menu Design Group, Inc.
(overall concept), The Menu
Workshop (inserts)
DESIGNERS
W. Scott Mahr
Liz Kearney

With this menu, Canyon Ranch's objective was for their guests to experience innovative cuisine while educating them about their nutritional philosophy. At the same time they needed to include regional differences in the two property locations, one in Lenox, Massachusetts and the other in Tucson, Arizona. The menu design was created to complement the casual but elegant dining experience. Scott Mahr of The Menu Design Group in New York devised folders for the menu and designed the covers. Liz Kearney of The Menu Workshop in Seattle designed the slip-in sheets. A nutritional message that rotates every eight days is revealed on the back side of the menu.

Fashion in Bloom

RESTAURANT/OPERATOR
Nut Tree
Nut Tree, CA
YEAR OPENED
1921
DESIGN FIRM
Nut Tree Design
DESIGNERS
Michael Green and Daniel Salcedo
ILLUSTRATOR
Daniel Salcedo
PRINTER
Ulatis Creek Printing

The Nut Tree hosts special events throughout the year including fashion shows held the first Tuesday of every month from November through June. As with each of their events, special menus are created. They have 30 different menus in the Fashion Expression series, using different materials, including dried flowers, beads, and confetti. Since only small quantities are produced, these menus quickly become collector's items.

Field Day
Cocktails 2.50

Luncheon prices include one of the following special entrees, a loaf of Nut Tree bread and a choice of coffee or hot tea.

Entrées

Celestial Salmon 12.95
Morsels of salmon carefully nestled on a bed of fresh spinach and cheese, neatly wrapped in a blanket of delicate pastry, baked golden brown, regally set afloat on a champagne sauce and christened "Celestial Salmon".

Stir-Fried Beef 10.95
Thin slices of beef, seasoned with fresh ginger, shallots, soy, tomato and brandy, all quick-fried with tender asparagus and served with spicy rice.

Summer Toss 11.95
Roasted chicken, baked ham and Jarlsberg cheese julienned and laced with crisp lettuce, watercress, cucumbers, tomato and mushrooms. This delightful garden is drizzled with French dressing.

Nut Tree Wines

Chardonnay, 1984
Fifth 9.95

Sauvignon Blanc, 1984
Fifth 7.95

Cabernet Sauvignon, 1983
Fifth 9.95

White Zinfandel, 1986
Fifth 6.75

Desserts

Chocolate Celebration 2.95
A chocolate cookie crust topped with a thin strip of truffle filling, a layer of Mexican chocolate cream and whipped cream.

Paradise Tartlet 2.75
A delightful tart crusted with a short coconut and macadamia nut pastry, filled with a refreshing lime creme, all topped with tropical fruits and whipped cream.

Almond Butter Crunch Mousse 2.75
A delicate creamy caramel mousse spirited with Bailey's Irish Cream and layered with our very own Almond Butter Crunch candy.

CHAPTER

3

Now That's Italian!

Trattoria Spiga

RESTAURANT/OPERATOR
Trattoria Spiga
Italian Restaurant Group
Costa Mesa, CA
YEAR OPENED
1991
DESIGN FIRM
On The Edge
DESIGNER
Karyn Verdak
ART DIRECTOR
Jeff Gasper
PHOTOGRAPHER
Joe Mozdzen

Spiga in Italian translates literally to "wheat husk" and figuratively to "staff of life." The restaurant itself is located inside an upscale shopping mall.

Because of the unique layout of the restaurant, there was an even greater need to create strong graphics and design elements to define the space and give it personality. Mixing warm textural background colors with brightly painted umbrellas, awnings and chairs helped unify and delineate the space as well as attract passersby.

The menus contrast warm duotone photos of dried wheat husks with the same band of bright colors that comprise the decor. The back screened wheat image is a rustic and friendly graphic that is repeated on various elements contained in the restaurant's identity package.

Antonello Ristorante

RESTAURANT/OPERATOR
Antonello Ristorante
Italian Restaurant Group
Santa Ana, CA
DESIGN FIRM
On The Edge
DESIGNER
Joe Mozdzen
ART DIRECTOR
Jeff Gasper
ILLUSTRATOR
Karyn Verdak
PHOTOGRAPHER
Joe Mozdzen
PRINTER
United Business Systems

Owner Antonio Cagnolo wanted something new to update his menu and reflect the lighter dishes he had spent two years developing. The result is a 22-page souvenir menu consisting of treasured recipes, family collections, food tips, vendor articles, family photos from Italy, and an award-winning wine list.

The cover photo is a collection of authentic Italian images. In addition, antique paper was color-scanned, and its texture reproduced as a background. The menu complements the rustic, old-world charm and impeccable standards of the restaurant itself. This work of art is available as a souvenir for a $10 donation to The Food Distribution Center, a local charity. The menu and its sales have garnered considerable publicity and continue to function as a powerful marketing tool. This menu won Third Place in the 1992 NRA Contest for "Best Merchandising."

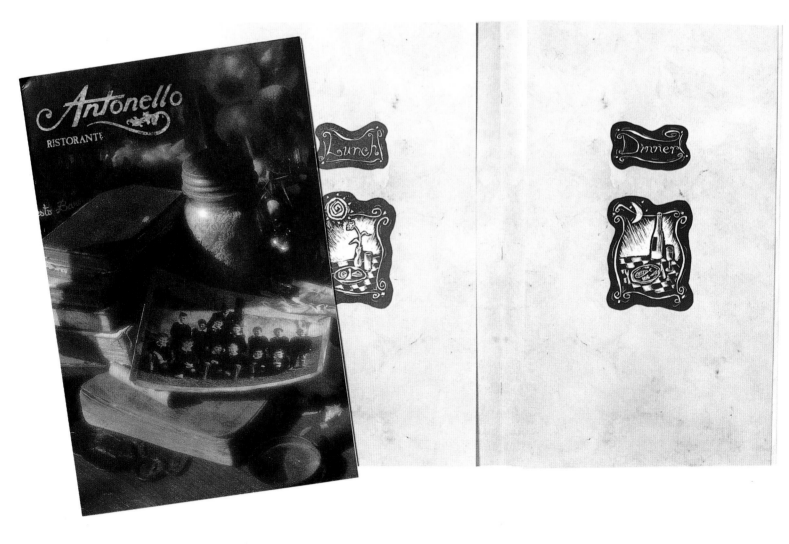

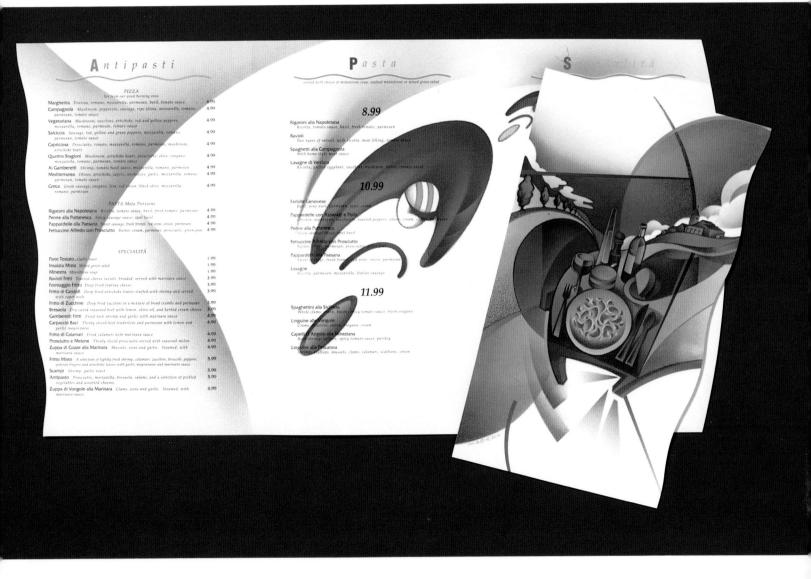

Baci Trattoria Lunch and Dinner

RESTAURANT/OPERATOR
Baci Trattoria/Gastronomy, Inc.
Salt Lake City, UT
YEAR OPENED
1989
DESIGN FIRM
Rob Magiera Illustration
DESIGNER
Rob Mageira
PRINTER
Quality Press

When restaurateurs from Gastronomy, Inc. conceived Baci, they imagined a marriage of fine art with fine food. The building's location in the heart of Salt Lake City's emerging Pierpont art and business district spurred the developers to integrate contemporary visual art into the restaurant. The restaurant gave the surrounding artistic community a chance to display their talents. Seven local artists were chosen, including painters, mixed media artists, graphic designers and a ceramicist. They were given two specifications: the work needed to be passionate and had to have an Italian theme. The result is an environment and aesthetic that one would expect to find only in Milan. The menu design is an accurate reflection of the restaurant's theme; it echoes the stained glass partition that separates the bar and private club from the public trattoria.

Baci won a Third Place in the 1992 NRA awards for "Best Design."

I Cugini

RESTAURANT/OPERATOR
I Cugini/
University Restaurant Group
Santa Monica, CA
YEAR OPENED
1990
DESIGN FIRM
Mary Oeffling Design
DESIGNER
Mary Oeffling
PRINTER
Castle Press

The name for this restaurant is based on the story of its two owners who are cousins. The menu is set up like a book to tell their story. The authentic and rustic quality is enhanced through the use of parchment paper and romance text. A chipboard cover features the owners as boys playing in the open air market of a small Italian city. The type style and the spot illustrations of fruits and vegetables reflect this Italian heritage. The interior elements of the restaurant—lighting, trompe l'oeil, faux frescoed walls, plants in terra cotta pots and the use of warm colors simulate the ambience of a traditional Italian restaurant. Patrons sitting on the terrace overlooking the Pacific Ocean can well imagine they are in a small coastal Italian village. Italian-style music, service and foods have all been closely adhered to.

Campagna

RESTAURANT/OPERATOR
Campagna/Ottima Idea Corporation
Telluride, CO
YEAR OPENED
1990
DESIGN FIRM
Marcia Heffering
DESIGNER
Marcia Heffering
ART DIRECTOR
Vincent Esposito (Ottima Idea Corporation)

Campagna, a Tuscan-style restaurant uses a menu that is handmade on the premises. A rooster, a classic country symbol, graphically represents the restaurant. Surrounding the rooster is an irregular pattern of mossaic blocks reminiscent of Italian medieval wood-block printing. Italian Fabriano paper, rustic in feel, is torn to create a deckle-edged menu folder. It is then handsomely imprinted with a custom-made rubber stamp. The personalized look is further realized by hand blending the ink colors; each becomes an original work of art. The folders, which accommodate a daily changing menu, receive a light coat of polyurethane spray to protect them, without giving a plastic appearance.

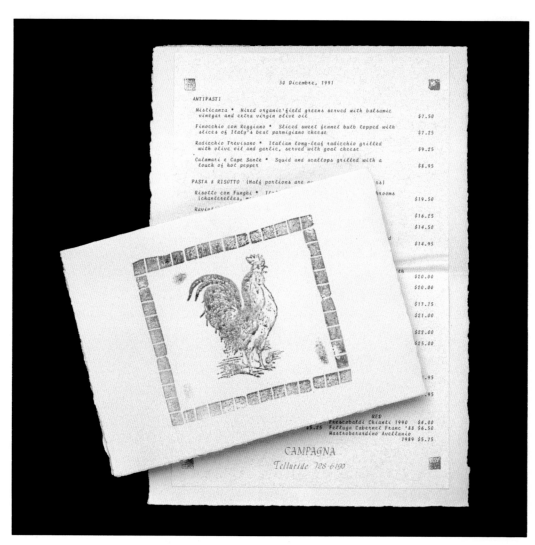

Spiaggia

RESTAURANT/OPERATOR
**Spiaggia/The Levy Organization
Chicago, IL**
YEAR OPENED
1984
DESIGN FIRM
**The Levy Organization—in house
creative services**
DESIGNER
Marcy Lansing
ILLUSTRATOR
Bobbye Cochran
PRINTER
Printing Arts, Inc.

Spiaggia in Chicago combines a
spectacular view of Lake Michigan
with authentic Northern Italian cuisine.
The resulting sophistication is apparent
in the elegant menu graphic with its
unconventional rendering of a Roman
column, wine glass and bottle, and
various foods. The outer shell of the
dinner menu remains constant, while
the insert is revised as often as
necessary. Bright colors adorn the
"specials" card used at lunch.

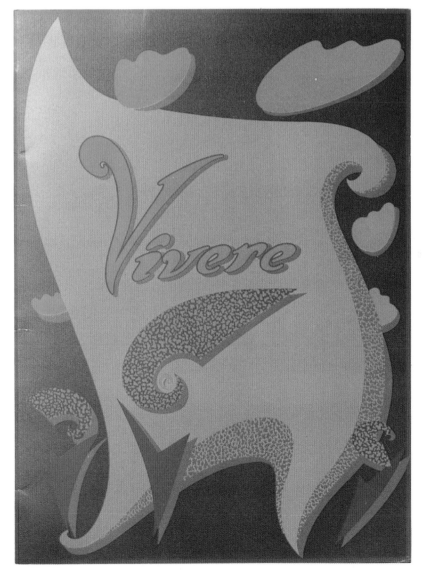

Vivere

RESTAURANT/OPERATOR
**Vivere/Italian Village
Restaurants Inc.
Chicago, IL**
YEAR OPENED
1990
DESIGN FIRM
Jordan Mozer & Associates
DESIGNER
Jordan Mozer

Vivere is an exotic dining room in
Chicago's Italian Village Restaurant,
an establishment that has been in the
Capitanini family for three generations.
Restaurant designer Jordan Mozer was
commissioned to give it a new look.
The space has a contemporary feel, yet
evokes the aura of the past. Mozer
wanted it to have an unexpected
personality, one that confuses ancient
and modern. Virtually everything in
Vivere is handmade or produced from
Mozer's freehand drawings enlarged to
life size. This explains why the space
looks as if it came out of an animated
film sketch.

The menu cover, inspired by Italian
architecture, sports free form shapes,
and spans the color palette with green
and black contrasting with terra cotta
and burnt orange.

Palio D'Asti

RESTAURANT/OPERATOR
Palio D'Asti
San Francisco, CA
YEAR OPENED
1990
DESIGN FIRM
Melanie Doherty Design
DESIGNER
Melanie Doherty
PRINTER
Western Deluna Press

The theme of the restaurant is based on the "Palio," a medieval bareback horse race and the regional culinary festival held annually in the Northern Italian hillside town of Asti. The colors represent the different participants of the race—the gold and black are from traditional costumes, the typography is based on calligraphy, and the "L" in the logo is a furlough marker. The mood of this medieval celebraton is clearly captured through graphics used on the menu, matches, wine label, shopping bag, stationery and take-out packaging.

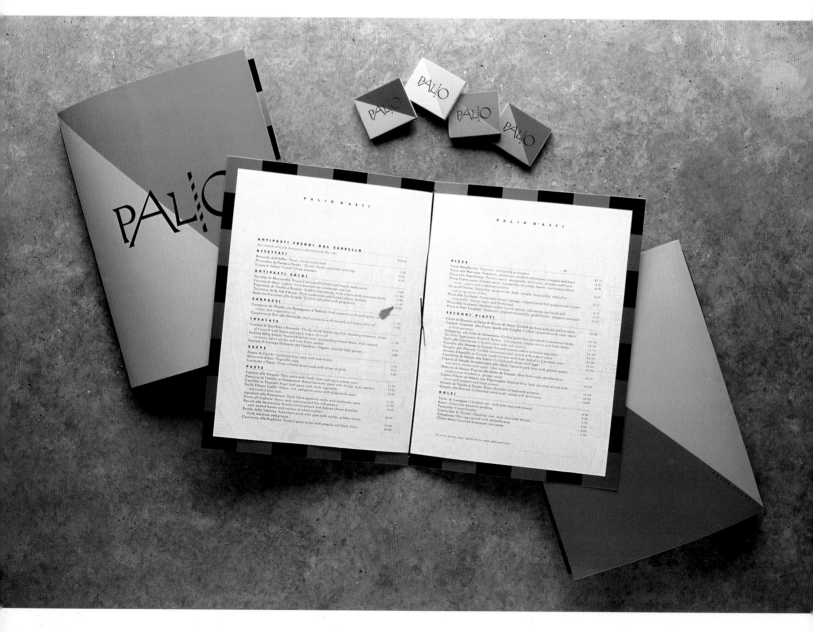

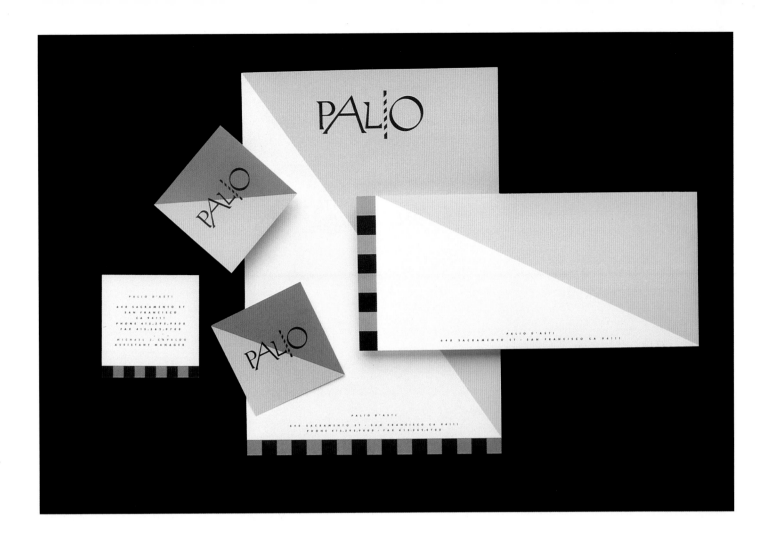

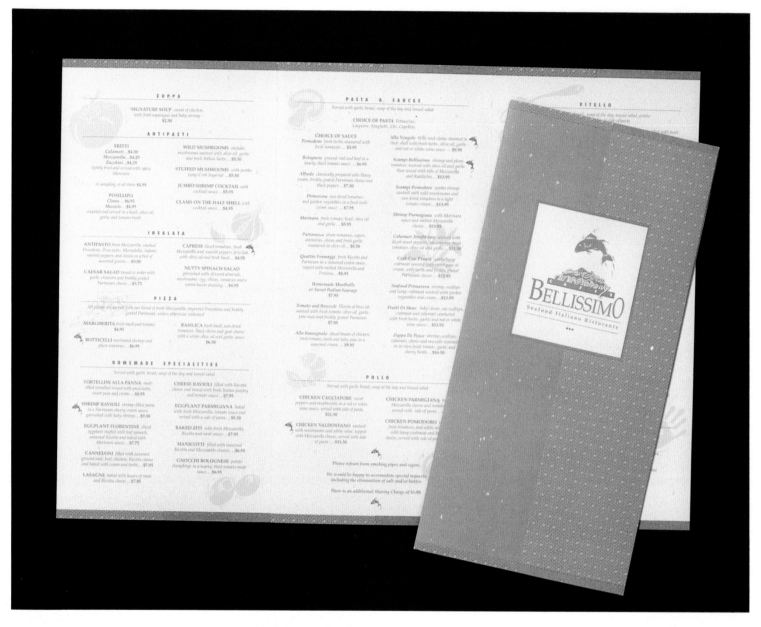

Caffe Bellissimo

RESTAURANT/OPERATOR
Caffe Bellissimo
Wilmington, DE
YEAR OPENED
1990
DESIGN FIRM
Ross Design Inc.
DESIGNERS
Tony Ross, Jen Walker,
June Sidwell
ART DIRECTOR
Tony Ross
ILLUSTRATOR
June Sidwell
PRINTER
Modern Press

Using patterns derived from the interior furnishings, the graphics for this menu design are tied directly into the fun and casually elegant decor. The coordinated identity system consists of take-out menus, letterhead, cocktail napkins, gift certificates, and the main menu. All are tastefully designed and produced using two-color ink combinations.

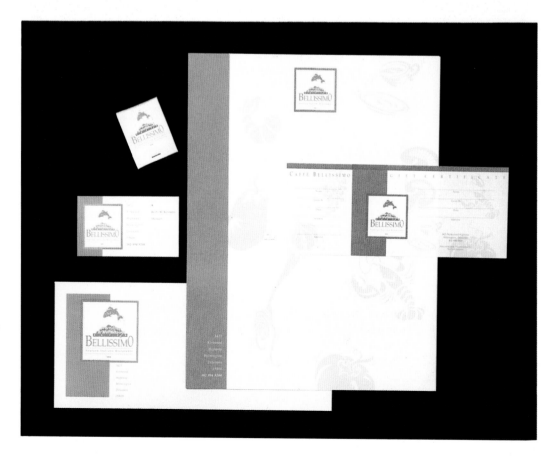

Luna Notte

RESTAURANT/OPERATOR
Luna Notte
San Antonio, TX
YEAR OPENED
1991
DESIGN FIRM
HIXO, Inc.
DESIGNER
Mike Hicks
PRINTER
Sterling Kwik Kopy

At Luna Notte the designer set out to create a graphics package that would separate this high-tech Italian restaurant design from the typical checkered tablecloth operation. It was designed to convey the modernism of the food operation, the authentic nature of the recipes, and to warrant at a higher price point. The architecture, signage and graphic elements, all developed from a single perspective, are consistent.

RESTAURANT/OPERATOR
Edwardo's Natural Pizza
Hillside, IL
YEAR OPENED
1978
DESIGN FIRM
Debra Schneider Designs
DESIGNER
Debra Schneider
PHOTOGRAPHER
Charles Shotwell
PRINTER
Bradley Printing
PAPER
laminated

At Edwardo's "fresh and natural" are not just words, but a commitment. Quality and freshness are the basis for the look of their menu design as well. The white-tiled background with its black border creates a clean canvas on which to feature the colorful fresh ingredients. It also ties in with the chain's Eurostyle decor. The abundance of fresh meats, cheese and vegetables exquisitely photographed and featured on the front and back covers are the same quality used in the restaurant's kitchen. The menu's interior is clean, colorful and up-beat to reflect the dining environment. Red and green relate to Edwardo's logo with yellow accents adding a splash of excitement. The color and shapes of each food item draw the eye through the menu, while guiding the customer to focus on the restaurant's popular and appealing selections.

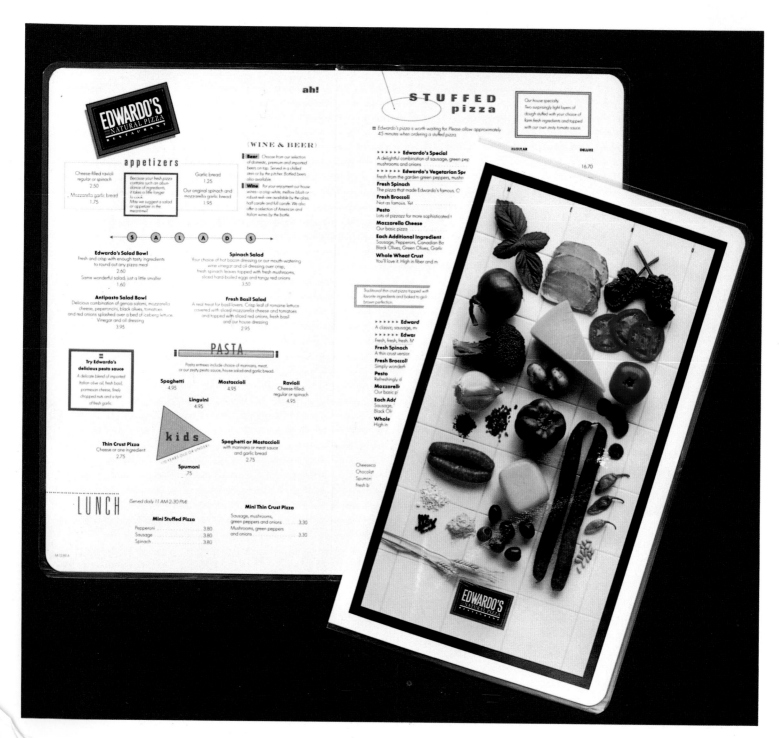

Capriccio Dinner

RESTAURANT/OPERATOR
Capriccio
The Peabody Orlando Hotel
Orlando, FL
YEAR OPENED
1986
DESIGN FIRM
Cleveland Menu Printing Co.
DESIGNER/ILLUSTRATOR
Carole Moy
PRINTER
Cleveland Menu Printing Co.

The cover illustration dramatically captures the essence of Capriccio's decor. Massive columns, black-and-white marble floors, green tabletops, and huge ceiling high windows covered with linen-colored Roman shades, are some of the distinctive interior elements of this upscale Northern Italian restaurant. One of the impressive features of the restaurant is a glass enclosed walk-in wine cellar and a wine list with over 230 selections.

Sfuzzi Menu Series

RESTAURANT/OPERATOR
Sfuzzi/Sfuzzi, Inc.
New York, NY
YEAR OPENED
1988
DESIGN FIRM
David Carter Graphic Design
DESIGNER
Randall Hill
ILLUSTRATOR
Kelly Stribling Southerland
PRINTER
Riverside Press

Sfuzzi is a national chain of Italian restaurants designed by architect Paul Draper. Each has its own distinctive personality yet all are part of a consistent image. The individual restaurants all have their own trademark frieze indicative of their particular location. This concept is subtly translated to include the menu design by using background patterns of torn handmade paper that relates to the frieze. Illustrations are lighthearted and fun, like the menu selections and the overall dining experience.

Louise's Trattoria

RESTAURANT/OPERATOR
**Louise's Trattoria
Santa Monica, CA**
YEAR OPENED
1985
DESIGN FIRM
James Weiner Design
DESIGNER
Jennifer Boose
PRINTER
Alan Lithograph

Louise's Trattoria was purchased in 1985 from a mom and pop operation. In its expansion and further concept development, the graphics and restaurant design were subsequently refined. The graphics needed to reflect Louise's interest in providing freshly made California-style Italian cuisine in a medium price range. They wanted to avoid a homogenized appearance, so the Louise's Trattoria corporate logo and overall restaurant design emphasize their commitment to fresh homemade

fare for the budget conscious diner. The original watercolor artwork used for the menu and the use of different colors and finishes in each restaurant's interior produce an overall effect of handcrafted comfort, yet with individual style.

The restaurant's interior makes use of natural finish materials and lively colors to create depth and visual interest by merging and intersecting architectural planes and solids. The corporate logo, again through use of color and merging planes, reflects this feeling of depth. The logo was recently adapted to express Louise's continuing interest in the handcrafted and artistic. The spirited colors and the hand-painted design combine name recognition with a consistent aesthetic look, but without sacrificing the ambience and impression of a neighborhood restaurant.

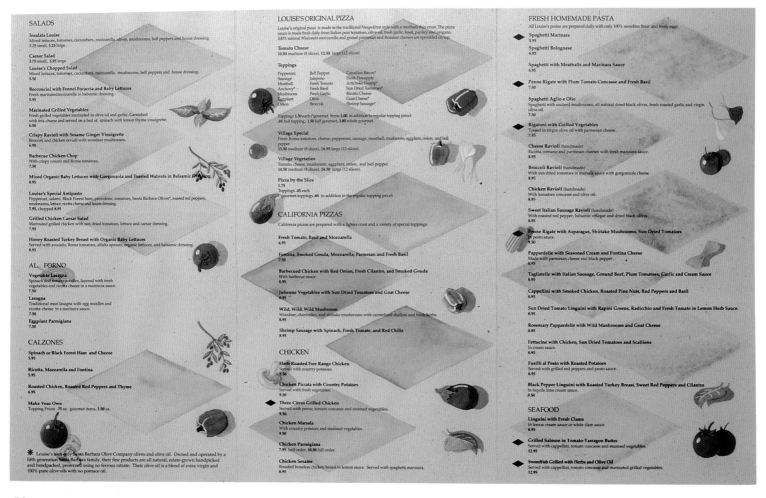

Pane e Vino

RESTAURANT/OPERATOR
Pane e Vino
Los Angeles, CA
YEAR OPENED
1991
DESIGN FIRM
Rod Dyer Group, Inc.
DESIGNER
Rod Dyer
ILLUSTRATOR
Rod Dyer

The menu's cover art lends itself to Pane e Vino's theme that one can subsist on bread and wine. However, the restaurant offers more than that. This modern day trattoria serves an array of simply prepared tasty Italian dishes representing the various regions of Italy.

Pane e Vino has three locations in California; the first opened in Santa Barbara with subsequent locations in San Francisco and Los Angeles. The Los Angeles location is graphic designer Rod Dyer's first venture as a

restaurateur. The menu presentation is a simple two-color postcard affixed to a coverstock and inserted into a black trimmed plastic cafe cover. Inside, the flexible menu format presents the customer with a clean concise selection of items to order. The Pane e Vino in Los Angeles also has available a "Porta a Casa," or food-to-go menu, that is in harmony with the restaurant's graphic style. This is a good way to offer customers a take-out option and limits the problem of stolen menus.

50   C I N Q V A N T A

Cinquanta

RESTAURANT/OPERATOR
Cinquanta
New York, NY
YEAR OPENED
1992
DESIGN FIRM
Presentations Ltd.
DESIGNER
Mario Pulice
ART DIRECTOR
Thomas Vlahakis
ILLUSTRATOR
Mario Pulice
PRINTER
F & T Graphics

Cinquanta, "50" in Italian, is the perfect name for this restaurant located at 50 East 50th Street in Manhattan. The restaurant itself is upscale in taste and style, as is its Midtown location. The concept for the menu design was derived from an all black floor-to-ceiling interior wall mural. An image from the mural is suggested on the cover by alternating matte black ink and matte varnish over a double pass of high gloss black finish. The final touch is an accent of metallic gold trim.

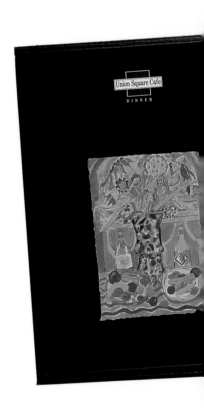

Union Square Cafe

RESTAURANT/OPERATOR
Union Square Cafe
New York, NY
YEAR OPENED
1985
DESIGNER
Danny Meyer
ILLUSTRATOR
Richard Polsky

Nearly every wall in the restaurant is adorned with artwork, even some three-dimensional pieces. The idea was to capture and carry the same feeling into the menu cover. The menu itself, is cleanly styled like the restaurant. There are a number of categories to choose from, all in a particular order. For instance, in addition to the regular menu, the weekly specials are listed on the bottom left and the daily specials on the bottom right. This allows customers an opportunity to play with the menu in many ways. They can choose to order a multi-course meal or simply order a sampling of appetizers. Napkin rings are printed from the same artwork and add a touch of panache to the tabletop. Postcards of the restaurant's artwork are available and if the customers wish to, they can take a bit of the experience home with them. Proprietor Danny Meyer believes that, "the more comfortable customers are, the happier they will be with the whole dining experience."

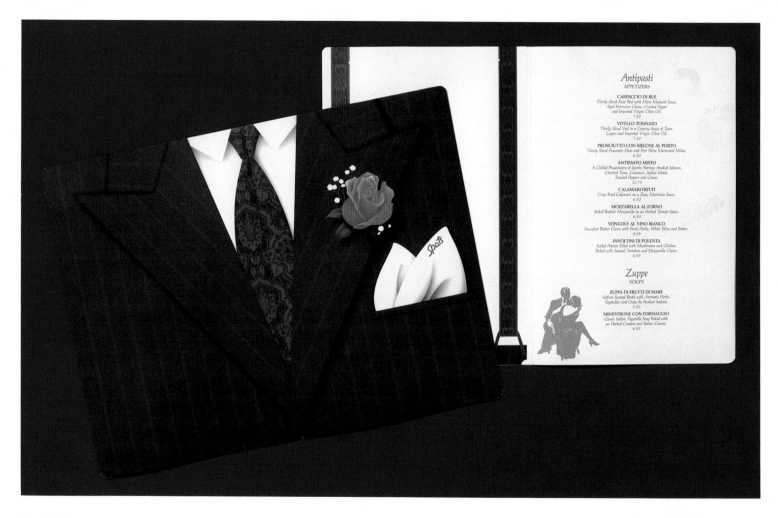

Spats Dinner

RESTAURANT/OPERATOR
**Spats/Hyatt Regency Maui
Lahaina, HI**
DESIGN FIRM
Kenyon Press
DESIGNER
Richard Witt
ILLUSTRATOR
Richard Witt
PRINTER
Kenyon Press

This unique tuxedo menu conveys the class and sophistication of Maui's well known Spats restaurant and nightclub. The client requested a contemporary design, one capable of housing a special wine list insert that would make a stylish statement. The illustration is a mock up of the floor manager's uniform. The suspenders on the inside cover are die-cut to hold the laser printed wine list insert.

What makes the design so clever, is that when the menu cover is opened and held by the customer, they appear to be wearing a rose-embellished tuxedo.

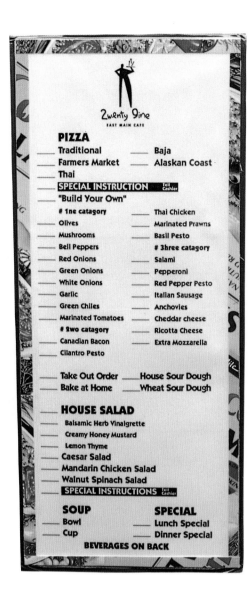

PIZZA
___ Traditional	___ Baja
___ Farmers Market	___ Alaskan Coast
___ Thai	

___ **SPECIAL INSTRUCTION** Tell Cashier

___ "Build Your Own"

___ # 1ne catagory	___ Thai Chicken
___ Olives	___ Marinated Prawns
___ Mushrooms	___ Basil Pesto
___ Bell Peppers	___ # 3hree catagory
___ Red Onions	___ Salami
___ Green Onions	___ Pepperoni
___ White Onions	___ Red Pepper Pesto
___ Garlic	___ Italian Sausage
___ Green Chiles	___ Anchovies
___ Marinated Tomatoes	___ Cheddar cheese
___ # 2wo catagory	___ Ricotta Cheese
___ Canadian Bacon	___ Extra Mozzarella
___ Cilantro Pesto	

___ Take Out Order	___ House Sour Dough
___ Bake at Home	___ Wheat Sour Dough

HOUSE SALAD
___ Balsamic Herb Vinaigrette
___ Creamy Honey Mustard
___ Lemon Thyme
___ Caesar Salad
___ Mandarin Chicken Salad
___ Walnut Spinach Salad

___ **SPECIAL INSTRUCTIONS** Tell Cashier

SOUP	**SPECIAL**
___ Bowl	___ Lunch Special
___ Cup	___ Dinner Special

BEVERAGES ON BACK

2wenty 9ine
EAST MAIN CAFE
29 E. Main Street, Los Gatos   395-4889

ESPRESSO BAR
___ House Coffee
___ Espresso
___ Cappuccino
___ Caffe Latte
___ Caffe Mocha
___ Mocha Chai
___ Single
___ Double
___ Decaffeinated
___ Take-out
___ Nonfat

___ **SPECIAL INSTRUCTIONS** Tell Cashier

BLENDER BAR
___ Pacific Lime Cooler
___ Club Cooler
___ Blitzen Berry
___ Orangeana
___ Wild Strawberry
___ Berry Orange
___ Power Lean Shake
___ Take-Out

___ **SPECIAL INSTRUCTIONS** Tell Cashier

___ **DESSERTS**
___ Gelato
___ Sorbetto

FOOD ON BACK

---

29 East Main Cafe

RESTAURANT/OPERATOR
29 East Main Cafe
Los Gatos, CA
YEAR OPENED
1992
DESIGN FIRM
Max Davis Company N.A.
DESIGNER
Max Davis
ILLUSTRATORS
Peter Lindberg, Max Davis,
Janis Anzalone

29 East Main Cafe is a small gourmet pizza, espresso and blender bar "hangout." The interior was done on a small budget and amounts to a collection of eclectic pieces, old and new, that have taken on new functions. Copper piping is used as an accent throughout the restaurant. The main menu is written on butcher paper. It is easily updated by tearing the old menu off and rewriting the new one. A wooden hutch is used to display food. As customers enter they may view the daily specials on the vibrantly painted hutch. This display was designed to create a fun visual preview of the fine foods offered and to hasten the ordering process. A small laminated menu was also designed to speed ordering. It allows the patrons to mark off their choices with a grease pencil. This menu's design reinforces the concept of homemade gourmet food. By recycling the ingredient packaging used in the food production, a colorful border treatment was created.

Red Tomato

RESTAURANT/OPERATOR
Red Tomato
Chicago, IL
YEAR OPENED
1990
DESIGN FIRM
Joed Design Marketing
Communications
DESIGNERS
Joe and Ed Rebek
ILLUSTRATOR
Dave Voigt (menus only)

The name Red Tomato implies ripeness. Elements of the logo and supporting graphics are used to reinforce this overall image. The objective of the restaurant was to have the designers create an identity and subsequent program that was unique and fun, yet versatile. The logo embodies this by using casually perpendicular words, varying letterscale and a trademark Italian plum tomato cartoon. An effort was made not to overuse the logo by applying it to everything in sight. With this in mind, a variety of supporting graphics that include a single tomato, other floating tomatoes and a juggling lady in flight add contrast but provide visual continuity.

CHAPTER
4
Americana

J.J. Musky's

RESTAURANT/OPERATOR
J.J. Musky's Eatery at Pipe Creek
Sandusky, OH
YEAR OPENED
1990
DESIGN FIRM
Hetland Ltd.
DESIGNER
Douglas J. Fliss
ILLUSTRATOR
Gary Baune
PHOTOGRAPHER
Rus Hanson
PRINTER
Foss Printing

The legend of J.J. Musky, a larger-than-life character, was created specifically as an identity for this restaurant. Many elements of J.J. Musky's lifestyle are used in the restaurant's interior. In fact, the restaurant encourages its patrons' participation by inviting them to donate bits and pieces of J.J. Musky ''memorabilia'' to the restaurant's museum. This scrapbook style menu contains handwritten notes and observations from J.J. himself.

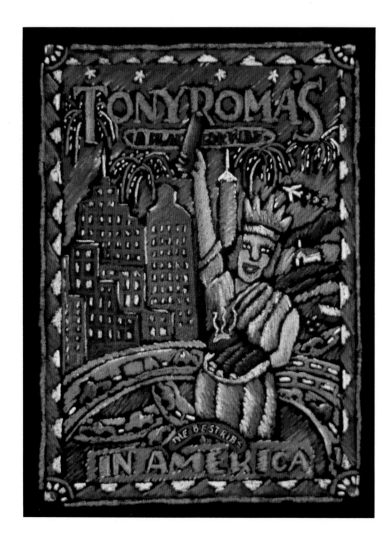

Prototype menu series
for Tony Roma's

RESTAURANT/OPERATOR
Tony Roma's/Roma Corporation
Dallas, TX
DESIGN FIRM
Dennard Creative
DESIGNER
Bob Dennard
ILLUSTRATORS
Covers: Chris Wood & June Michel
Inside Spreads: James Lacey

Tony Roma's is known for serving,
"the best ribs in America." Using that
as a starting point, a series of
whimsical menu cover prototypes were
created with American style imagery as
the design basis. The illustrations
created for this series are of the Statue
of Liberty, Uncle Sam, a cowboy, and
an astronaut. The idea was to
communicate to the customer that no
matter where they are, West, Midwest,
or even New York City, the best ribs
can be found at Tony Roma's. The
concept included framed posters of
each cover. Unfortunately, these
prototypes were never produced.

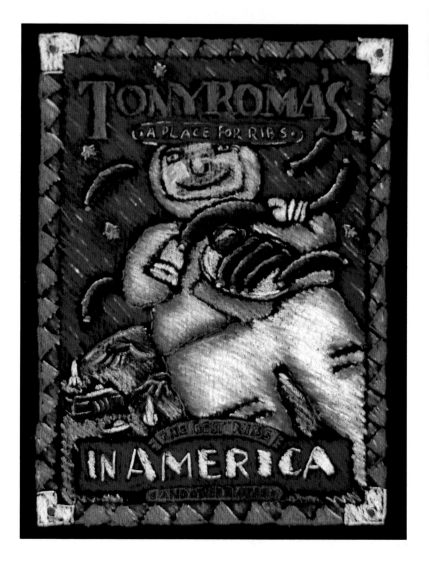

Cromwell's Tavern

RESTAURANT/OPERATOR
Cromwell's Tavern
Greenville, DE
YEAR OPENED
1991
DESIGN FIRM
Ross Design
DESIGNER
June Sidwell
ART DIRECTOR
Tony Ross
ILLUSTRATOR
June Sidwell
PRINTER
Diamond Printing

Through use of traditional color and woodcut techniques, this menu design communicates a classic colonial feel with a contemporary twist. It is a rich presentation considering the designer used only two colors on recycled paper.

Country Kitchen

RESTAURANT/OPERATOR
Country Kitchen
Country Hospitality Corp.
Minneapolis, MN
YEAR OPENED
1950
DESIGN FIRM
Baker & Grooms
DESIGNER
Mikie Baker
ILLUSTRATOR
Joe Spencer
PRINTER
Reynolds Printing
MATERIAL
Teslin Synthetic Printing Sheet by PPG Industries

The Country Kitchen wanted to communicate a homey look that was classic in feel, appearance and a departure from the previous menu which had featured food photography. They found the look they wanted by using illustrations of stylized orange crate labels that were rendered to highlight food categories. The top of each page features a heading styled after a label. The Padgco cover and synthetic Teslin material were chosen to increase the menu's longevity in the high volume chain.

Country Kitchen was 1991 Third Place winner in the NRA's "Average Check Under $8" category.

Mitzel's

RESTAURANT/OPERATOR
**Mitzel's American Kitchen
Seattle, WA**
YEAR OPENED
1984
DESIGN FIRM
Spangler Associates
DESIGNER
Kathy Spangler
ART DIRECTOR
Ross Hogin
PHOTOGRAPHER
Don Mason
PRINTER
Lithocraft

Mitzel's specializes in homestyle meals served in a cozy atmosphere. Their decor is carefully orchestrated to insure a feeling of warmth and friendliness. The menu design is a visual representation of what one might expect to find on a visit to Grandma's house. The intent was to evoke the pleasant emotion associated with grandmothers, but it was important to the owners that it not appear to be too old fashioned.

By blending the old with the new, the menu is still a reflection of the modern family. The positioning statement, "Creating Traditions For Today," sums up Mitzel's approach. The cover uses a series of photographs in simple and ornate frames. New portraits, as well as old ones, were selected as a means of achieving the desired effect. One of the objectives of this design was for the menu to be flexible and easy to update. To accomplish this, full-color master sheets are preprinted in quantity and imprinted with two colors as needed.

Cornucopia

RESTAURANT/OPERATOR
Nut Tree
Nut Tree, CA
YEAR OPENED
1921
DESIGN FIRM
Nut Tree Design
DESIGNER
Daniel Salcedo
ILLUSTRATOR
Thompson & West, 1877
PRINTER
Ulatis Creek

Nut Tree is more than a restaurant. It is also the story of a pioneer California ranch owned and managed by one family for over five generations. Evolving from a fruit ranch into a renowned restaurant and adjoining shop, the Nut Tree extends hospitality to those traveling along Interstate 80 or the Sacramento Valley Fly Way. Today, the fifth generation of Josiah Allison's heirs are managing the operation.

This special menu entitled, "A Cornucopia of Solano County," is a celebration of the restaurant's historic past and its culinary present. The menu not only lists food selections, but is a hand bound scrapbook, drilled and string tied. It contains engraved maps of the local area dating back to 1877.

The Nut Tree was a 1992 NRA winner in the "Checks Over $15" category.

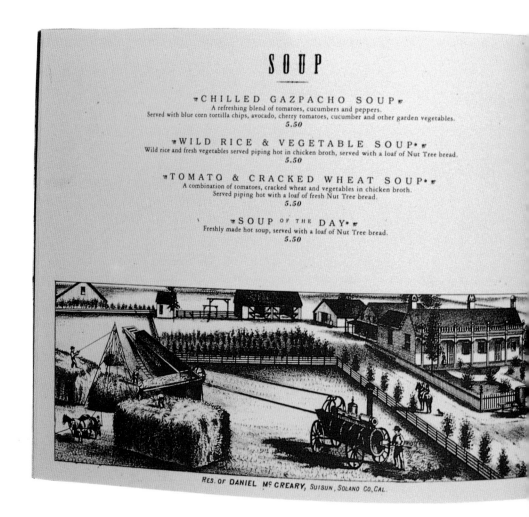

Stage Deli

RESTAURANT/OPERATOR
Stage Deli
Atlanta Restaurant Concepts
Atlanta, GA
YEAR OPENED
1991
DESIGN FIRM
In House
ART DIRECTOR
Barry Berlin
ILLUSTRATOR
Don G. Kingman

The Stage Deli, a Times Square landmark and destination for tourists and locals alike, captures the flavor of New York City. The menu cover features an illustration framed in marquee lighting and is symbolic of one of the most famous views of Times Square's traditional New Year's Eve countdown. The restaurant was built with the original look of the great delis of New York including a duplicate of a "New York long bar." The interior features dark woods, a black-and-white tile floor, a display kitchen, a takeout area, and a sit down counter.

STAGE DELI of New York

ATLANTA

LOS ANGELES   NEW YORK   CLEVELAND   BOSTON

NEW YORK'S BEST CORNED BEEF
"Over 50 Years"

APPETIZER SALADS

Served with an individual loaf of Nut Tree bread.

GARDEN GREEN SALAD *6.95*
Fresh greens, slices of tomatoes and cucumber topped with feta cheese.
Served with Nut Tree dressing.

ITALIAN VEGETABLE *6.95*
Marinated string beans with sliced mushrooms, zucchini, red onions and cherry tomatoes.
Served with fresh Creamy Italian dressing.

SPINACH SALAD *6.95*
Tender leaves of spinach gently tossed in a special Nut Tree dressing,
layered with thin slices of tomato and topped with crumbled bacon and feta cheese.

FRUIT SALAD *6.95*
A fanciful arrangement of fresh fruits and melons, topped with sherbet or cottage cheese.
Served with freshly baked nut bread and original Nut Tree marshmallow sauce.

ENDIVE & BAY SHRIMP SALAD *7.95*
Pacific Bay Shrimp arranged with Belgian endive and served with our special dressing.

"BUNKER HILL RANCH", RESIDENCE OF LEVI KORNS, VACA VALLEY, SOLANO CO., CAL.

Nut Tree 70th Anniversary

RESTAURANT/OPERATOR
Nut Tree
Nut Tree, CA
YEAR OPENED
1921
DESIGN FIRM
Nut Tree Design
DESIGNER
Daniel Salcedo
ILLUSTRATOR
Ray Ward
PRINTER
Ulatis Creek

From its beginnings as a humble
produce stand back in 1921, Nut Tree
has served as an oasis for weary
travelers. Will Rogers and Herbert
Hoover are among the restaurant's
many famous visitors. This
commemorative menu was designed to
celebrate their 70th anniversary. The
menu cover is a collage of memorabilia
and old photographs. Throughout the
menu are references to milestone years
in the restaurant's history. The menus
were produced in conjunction with an
advertising campaign using the same
imagery for consistency.

Carousel

RESTAURANT/OPERATOR
Carousel Coffee Shop & Deli
Tropworld Casino
Atlantic City, NJ
DESIGN FIRM
Associates
DESIGNER
Jill Varvil
PHOTOGRAPHER
stock photography
PRINTER
Associates

The location of Carousel, an Atlantic
City coffee shop and deli, was the
main inspiration for the playful design
of this menu. Its cover photograph of
a merry-go-round reminds us of a
bygone era. The historic aspects of the
Boardwalk lend themselves to nostalgia
as well, and are reflected in the
photographs displayed throughout the
restaurant's interior.

Hot & Cold Entrées

The Nut Tree features a selection of one-plate meals which combine a hot entrée with chilled tropical fruits and vegetables. Served with an individual loaf of Nut Tree bread.

Golden Prawns with Tropical Fruit 11.95
Golden fried prawns arranged with chilled fresh pineapple, papaya, avocado, banana and tomato slices with our Tropical dressing.

Nut Tree Tamale* 11.95
A large homemade corn husk turkey tamale with avocado, sour cream, sliced tomato and wedges of Jack cheese.

Chicken Curry with Mandarin Fruit* 10.95
Boneless chicken combined with an Indian curry sauce and served on rice. Condiments of bean sprouts and orange slices, coconut, cashews and chutney make this a hearty favorite.

Breast of Chicken with Tropical Fruit* 10.95
Half breast of chicken in chunks of white meat arranged with chilled fresh pineapple, papaya, avocado, banana and tomato slices with our Tropical dressing.

Green Pasta & Vegetables 9.95
Spinach lettuce and vegetables topped with tomato sauce and Italian Asiago cheese served with seasonal fruit.

1922

a restaurant was constructed, and the Nut Tree divided its hot menu. Hundreds of menus later, we still perpetuate the same tradition of quality, serving only the freshest fruits and vegetables and selecting only the finest ingredients for our homemade breads, pastries and exotic desserts.

Entrée Salads

Entrée salads served with a loaf of Nut Tree bread and butter.

Fresh Fruit Plate 11.95 Medium 13.95 Large
An assortment of fresh pineapple, papaya, banana, coconut, oranges and other seasonal fruits. Served with a loaf of nut bread and a choice of cottage cheese, sherbet or Nut Tree ice cream.

Breast of Chicken Salad 11.95
Chilled slices of smoked chicken with fresh basil dressing arranged upon butter lettuce and endive surrounded by tropical fruits.

Pacific Bay Shrimp Salad 13.95
Bay shrimp from the Pacific Northwest, Belgian endive, avocado, tomato and cucumber with French dressing.

1932

By the year 1932 the Nut Tree had become an established Western institution that hosted such famous Americans as Will Rogers and President Herbert Hoover. In the seventy years since, the Nut Tree has been host to five presidents, several governors, countless senators, multitudes of dignitaries, the Queen of Great Britain – and you.

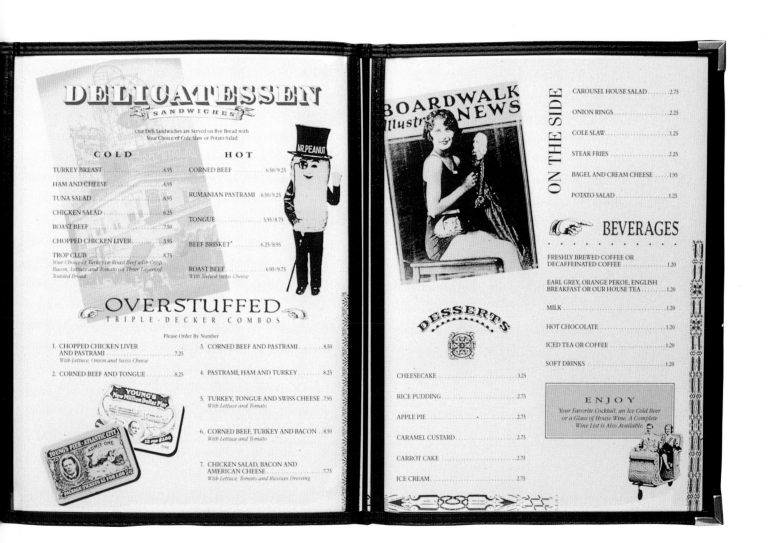

CHAPTER
5

Unique Materials

Humu Humu Nuku Nuku Apua'a

RESTAURANT/OPERATOR
**Grand Hyatt Wailea
Maui, HI**
DESIGN FIRM
Associates
DESIGNER
Beth Finn
PRINTER
Associates
MATERIAL
Koa wood

Taking its name from a Hawaiian fish, the client wanted to use simple materials with a native feel. Primitive etchings were burned into the native koa wood used in the construction of this menu. The complete system includes dinner and dessert menus, a wine list, and the private cellar menu. There is also an extensive 44 page drink menu complete with descriptive copy and illustrations of each offering. As a special treat, the Luau award is used for gift certificates.

This menu won a Second Place award in the "Specialty" category of the NRA's 1992 Great Menu contest.

Gampy's

RESTAURANT/OPERATOR
Gampy's
Baltimore, MD
YEAR OPENED
1978
DESIGN FIRM
The Menu Design Group, Inc.
DESIGNER
W. Scott Mahr
ILLUSTRATOR
Nancy Tive
PRINTER
B.C. Lucas Printers
MATERIAL
corplas plastic

Since Gampy's menu was so extensive it had to be large, and because many items are subject to frequent change it also needed to be flexible. The designer combined Pop Art styling with neon colors on a futuristic corplas cover. The result is a menu that is both kitsch and cool. Designed in sections, each is housed in its own pocket accommodating a slip-in-sheet; this design made it easy to update. If shrimp prices rise, they need only imprint the seafood area. The four-color backgrounds were printed as masters, and all the menu items are laser printed on an "as needed" basis.

The Algonquin

RESTAURANT/OPERATOR
Rose Room/The Algonquin Hotel
New York, NY
YEAR OPENED
1902
DESIGN FIRM
The Menu Design Group, Inc.
DESIGNER
W. Scott Mahr
PRINTER
B.C. Lucas

The Algonquin, undergoing a complete renovation, wanted to recapture the spirit of the original hotel. The problem was that The Rose Room, its well known dining room, had no logo. The designer set out to create one that reflected both the period and contained elements of contemporary design. The menu was fabricated to look like a hard cover book, a reference to the Algonquin Round Table, a group of writers who used to meet there. The cover is decorated with a dried, pressed rosebud appliqued to handmade paper. Inside, the menu items are printed on a textured stock that imitates handmade paper. The soft pink color of the menu coordinates with the room's decor.

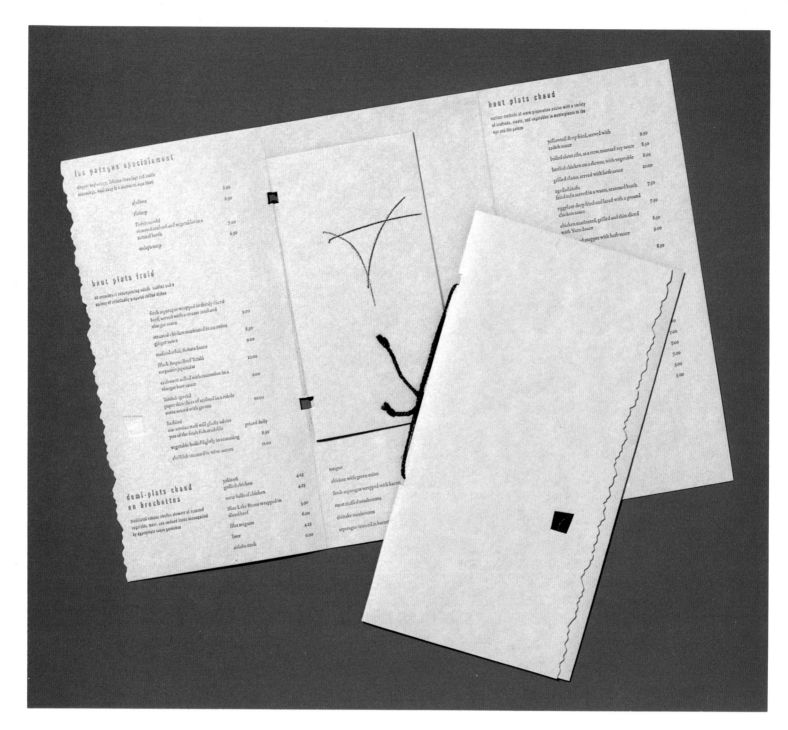

Robata Restaurant

RESTAURANT/OPERATOR
Robata Restaurant
Beverly Hills, CA
YEAR OPENED
1989
DESIGN FIRM
COY, Los Angeles
DESIGNER
Sean Alatorre
ART DIRECTOR
John Coy
PRINTER
Anderson Printing
MATERIAL
Kimberly Clark Buckskin

The rough-hewn edge of the menu reflects the raw granite used in Robata's interior. The objective to the menu design was to find a distinctive and elegant solution to accommodate a unique menu selection system. A durable synthetic, almost leather-like material with a velvety feel was used. The refined Robata logo is hot foil stamped in matte black and accented with a hand tied, fabric cord that holds the insert pages in place.

Aldo Baldo

RESTAURANT/OPERATOR
Aldo Baldo/Big 4 Restaurants
Phoenix, AZ
YEAR OPENED
1990
DESIGN FIRM
Cornoyer Hedrick
DESIGNER
Michon Jablonski
ART DIRECTOR
Idie McGinty
MATERIAL
aluminum

Not only is Aldo Baldo's menu sturdy, it's bulletproof. It was developed to enhance the restaurant's theme of an eccentric inventor's workshop and warehouse. It comes complete with surreal explanatory text on the back.

The metal cover and rings that hold the pages have an industrial quality. The interior pages are prepared in small quantities on pre-printed stationery that can be inserted into acetate pockets housed inside the aluminum covers.

This menu won First Place in the ''Most Imaginative'' category of the 1991 NRA Awards.

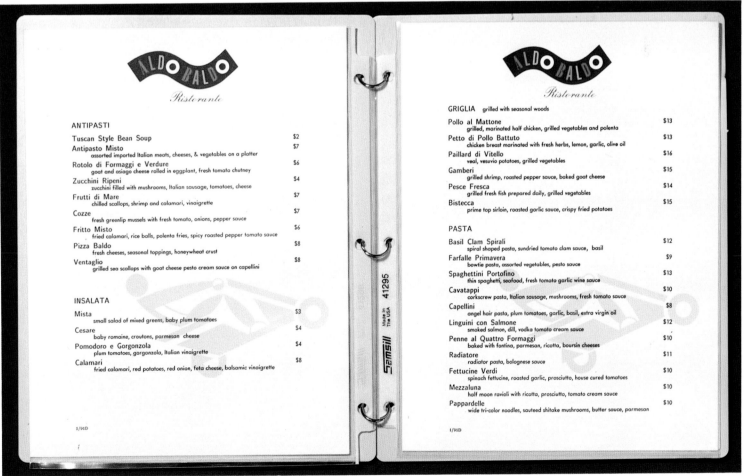

ANTIPASTI

Tuscan Style Bean Soup	$2
Antipasto Misto	$7
assorted imported Italian meats, cheeses, & vegetables on a platter	
Rotolo di Formaggi e Verdure	$6
goat and asiago cheese rolled in eggplant, fresh tomato chutney	
Zucchini Ripeni	$4
zucchini filled with mushrooms, Italian sausage, tomatoes, cheese	
Frutti di Mare	$7
chilled scallops, shrimp and calamari, vinaigrette	
Cozze	$7
fresh greenlip mussels with fresh tomato, onions, pepper sauce	
Fritto Misto	$6
fried calamari, rice balls, polenta fries, spicy roasted pepper tomato sauce	
Pizza Baldo	$8
fresh cheeses, seasonal toppings, honeywheat crust	
Ventaglio	$8
grilled sea scallops with goat cheese pesto cream sauce on capellini	

INSALATA

Mista	$3
small salad of mixed greens, baby plum tomatoes	
Cesare	$4
baby romaine, croutons, parmesan cheese	
Pomodoro e Gorgonzola	$4
plum tomatoes, gorgonzola, Italian vinaigrette	
Calamari	$8
fried calamari, red potatoes, red onion, feta cheese, balsamic vinaigrette	

1/91D

GRIGLIA   grilled with seasonal woods

Pollo al Mattone	$13
grilled, marinated half chicken, grilled vegetables and polenta	
Petto di Pollo Battuto	$13
chicken breast marinated with fresh herbs, lemon, garlic, olive oil	
Paillard di Vitello	$16
veal, vesuvio potatoes, grilled vegetables	
Gamberi	$15
grilled shrimp, roasted pepper sauce, baked goat cheese	
Pesce Fresca	$14
grilled fresh fish prepared daily, grilled vegetables	
Bistecca	$15
prime top sirloin, roasted garlic sauce, crispy fried potatoes	

PASTA

Basil Clam Spirali	$12
spiral shaped pasta, sundried tomato clam sauce, basil	
Farfalle Primavera	$9
bowtie pasta, assorted vegetables, pesto sauce	
Spaghettini Portofino	$13
thin spaghetti, seafood, fresh tomato garlic wine sauce	
Cavatappi	$10
corkscrew pasta, Italian sausage, mushrooms, fresh tomato sauce	
Capellini	$8
angel hair pasta, plum tomatoes, garlic, basil, extra virgin oil	
Linguini con Salmone	$12
smoked salmon, dill, vodka tomato cream sauce	
Penne al Quattro Formaggi	$10
baked with fontina, parmesan, ricotta, boursin cheeses	
Radiatore	$11
radiator pasta, bolognese sauce	
Fettucine Verdi	$10
spinach fettucine, roasted garlic, prosciutto, house cured tomatoes	
Mezzaluna	$10
half moon ravioli with ricotta, prosciutto, tomato cream sauce	
Pappardelle	$10
wide tri-color noodles, sauteed shitake mushrooms, butter sauce, parmesan	

1/91D

PRIX FIXE

RESTAURANT/OPERATOR
Prix Fixe
1818 Culinary Enterprises Inc.
New York, NY
YEAR OPENED
1990
DESIGN FIRM
Louise Fili Ltd.
DESIGNER
Louise Fili
PHOTOGRAPHER
Marcia Lippman
PRINTER
Darby Printing
MATERIAL
Zander's Elephant Hide

As restaurants have been forced to address the recession, so have restaurant graphics. At Prix Fixe, simplicity was the key. Keeping that in mind, this restaurant was designed to capture the eclectic quality of the nouvelle cuisine. The interior of the restaurant is grand and elegant; the bar has been painted gold and two enormous crystal chandeliers rescued from the shuttered B. Altman department store enhance the interior design. The graphics sought to strike a balance, something that would fit with the restaurant's grand scale and, yet, remain functional. The logo is hot foil stamped on Zander's Elephant Hide paper for maximum contrast. The photographic image on the cover was reproduced in large quantities and hand tipped on. It was further used on napkin rings, and even postcards.

Coyote Grill

RESTAURANT/OPERATOR
Coyote Grill/PB & J Restaurants
Shawnee Mission, KS
YEAR OPENED
1990
DESIGN FIRM
Eilts Design
ILLUSTRATOR
Patrice Eilts
DESIGNER
Patrice Eilts
PRINTERS
Inserts: Insty Prints,
Silkscreen Cover: Cicero
de-boss: Ace Die
MATERIAL
Latex impregnated paper

The design for the Coyote Grill needed to communicate that it was an upscale restaurant featuring Southwestern cuisine. The interior makes use of light colors reminiscent of the desert. It is natural in feel, with terra cotta tiled floors, adobe walls, and succulents and cactus in terra cotta pots.

A durable latex impregnated paper gives the menu cover texture and a tactile appearance that mimics sand. Tied with a leather thong and knotted with a turquoise bead, the cover features two paw prints that make a simple statement.

S O U P S & S A N D W I C H E S

Tortilla Soup	Bowl 2.95 Cup 1.75	Soup Of The Day	Bowl 2.95 Cup 1.75

Ancho Chicken Salad 5.50
Smoked Chicken Tossed in a Garlic Ancho Mayonnaise and Served on Foccacia Bread.

Tuna Kahuna 5.50
It's Tuna Salad Our Way. Served on Whole Wheat Bread. Try It Once and You're Hooked.

Albuquerque Turkey 5.75
Smoked Turkey with Lettuce. Tomato. Avocado and Monterey Jack Cheese. Dressed with Cilantro Mayonnaise and Served on Whole Wheat Bread.

BLT 5.95
Smoked Thick Slab Bacon. Fresh Lettuce and Tomato Served on Toasted Foccacia Bread.

Soup and Sandwich 5.95
All the Above Sandwiches Are Available in Half Portions with Tortilla Soup or Soup of the Day.

Salad and Sandwich 6.95
All the Above Sandwiches Are Available in Half Portions with Your Choice of Spinach Salad. Southwest Caesar, Coyote Salad, Cory, Cobb or Taos.

CBS 6.95
Tune Into This Sandwich. It's Got A Lot To Offer. Grilled Chicken Breast. Plus Bacon. Plus Cheddar Cheese. Served on a Fresh Toasted Bun.

Smoked Chicken Club 6.25
Smoked Chicken, Monterey Jack Cheese, Bacon, Lettuce, Tomato with Ancho Chili Mayonnaise and Served on Foccacia Bread.

Sure Fire Chicken 6.25
Char-Broiled Chicken Breast with Southwest Seasoning. Topped with Monterey Jack Cheese and Coyote Barbecue Sauce on a Toasted Bun.

Steak Sandwich 6.95
Grilled Marinated Flank Steak Topped with Anaheim Chilis. Sauteed Mushrooms and Smoked Mozzarella Cheese. Served on Baguette Bread.

Hamburger Coyote 5.95
Lettuce, Tomato, Red Onion, and French Fried Potatoes With a Kosher Dill Pickle. Salad. Served with or without Cheese.

All Cold Sandwiches Served With Chips. All Hot Sandwiches Served With Fries

T A C O S

Pork Taco 6.95
Sauteed Marinated Pork Tossed with Mushrooms. Red Cabbage and Radish Sprouts. Rolled in Oriental Pancakes and Served with a Hoisin-Plum Sauce.

Chicken Taco 5.95
Smoked Chicken Tossed in a Barbecue Mole Sauce with Two Cheeses and Diced Tomatoes.

Veggie Taco 5.95
Grilled Marinated Peppers, Squash and Sundried Tomatoes topped with three cheeses.

The Other Chicken Taco 5.95
Vive Le Difference! Grilled Chicken with a Jalapeno Cilantro Sauce. Caciotta Cheese and Smoked Jalapeno Peppers.

All Items Served on Soft White Flour Tortillas.

ENTREES

lled Sunset Strip   *15.95*
*Oz Grilled Kansas City Strip Topped with a Molasses
ni-Glaze and Teamed up with a Compote of Smoked Ba-
Sweet Potatoes, Pearl Onions and Pecans. Served with
acco Onions.*

asted Chicken   *10.95*
*m Roasted Chicken Stuffed with Fresh Herb Goat
se. Served with Oven Roasted Vegetables and a Red
per Basil Broth.*

on Chicken   *11.95*
*rinated Double Breast of Chicken Topped with a Colorful
iety of Southwest Sauces. Served with Mashed Potatoes.*

Calamari Steak   *11.95*
*Calamari Steak Prepared Abalone Style Lightly Breaded
and Sauteed. Stuffed with Shrimp and a Blend of Cheeses.
Served on a Bed of Blue Corn Pasta with Cilantro Jalapeno Cream.*

Steppin' Out Trout   *9.95*
*Fresh Missouri Trout Rolled in Sunflower Seeds, Dried
Cranberries and Yellow Corn Meal with a Mint Scallion
Marigold Cream. Served with rice*

Filet And Stuffed Poblano   *15.95*
*Tenderloin of Beef Brushed with Ancho Chilies. Served
with a Chicken Stuffed Poblano Pepper Grilled to Order
and Served with Goat Cheese and Red Pepper Creams.*

Lamb-ada "The Forbidden Dish"   *16.95*
*Lamb Marinated with Fresh Rosemary and Garlic. Grilled
to Order and Served with a Garlic, Ginger Jalapeno Sauce.*

We Said, " DUCK!"   *14.95*
*Duck Mallard Served with a Dried Black Cherry Wild
Mushroom Demi-Glaze. Accompanied by Mashed Potatoes.*

Enchiladas
*wo Corn Tortillas with Red
tta Cheese and Tomatillo Cilantro Rissota*
95

Served With Salad or Soup

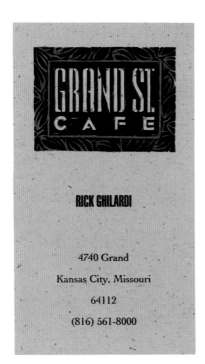

RICK GHILARDI

4740 Grand

Kansas City, Missouri

64112

(816) 561-8000

Grand Street Cafe

RESTAURANT/OPERATOR
Grand Street Cafe
PB & J Restaurants
Kansas City, MO
YEAR OPENED
1991
DESIGN FIRM
Muller and Company
DESIGNER
Patrice Eilts
ILLUSTRATORS
Rich Kobs/Patrice Eilts
PRINTER
Inserts: Insty Prints
MATERIAL
Cork

The graphics created for the Grand Street Cafe are a reflection of the sophisticated natural cuisine featured by the restaurant. Centered on the menu's cover, the logo with its leaf border, is an actual wood cut. It was silk screened in three colors that complement the restaurant's decor. The cover consists of cork paper laminated to kraft cover stock. It was chosen for its stain resistance as well as for its aesthetic qualitites. Because the food items change, the menu pages consist of four different colored inserts. These are bound between the cork cover and a laminated piece of chipboard for strength. A willow twig lashed with twine serves to hold all the pieces together and adds a natural touch. The wine list, printed on kraft cover stock, complements the menu. The scraps of cork left over from the menu cover were saved and used to make business cards. These were letter-pressed on the back and hand colored.

Cimarron

RESTAURANT/OPERATOR
**Cimarron/Brookhollow Marriott
Houston, TX**
YEAR OPENED
1991
DESIGN FIRM
Diana Delucia Design
DESIGNER
**Diana Delucia
and J. Duffy**
PRINTER
Brunswick
MATERIAL
Buckskin

The client, Cimarron, wanted help in creating an identity for their Southwestern-style restaurant. This unusually sized menu utilizes a synthetic leather-like paper stock with a rough cut edge. Bound with jute tied into a loose fitting bow, the cover features the restaurant's signature style logo. The interior pages, with a deckled edge, appear to overprint old maps of the Southwest.

Carmella's Cafe

RESTAURANT/OPERATOR
Carmella's Cafe
New Hartford, NY
YEAR OPENED
1985
DESIGN FIRM
Trainor Associates
DESIGNER
Gary Price
PHOTOGRAPHER
Larry Pacilio
PRINTER
Seattle Menu
MATERIAL
Teslin Synthetic Printing
Sheet by PPG Industries

Everything in Carmella's is designed to coordinate with the restaurant's nostalgia theme. The goal of the menu was to reflect the personality of the restaurant in printed form. It was meant to be a mirror of the restaurant's personality. A synthetic stock makes this menu extremely durable and easy to clean.

⬧DRINKS

Wine
Chardonnay, White Zinfandel, Cabernet Sauvignon.
By the Glass or Bottle.
House Wine Burgundy, Chablis, Blush. By the Glass or Carafe.

Beer
Heineken, Bud, Molson & Other Assorted Draft & Bottled Beer.
(23 oz Drafts too!)

Espresso
Cafe Authentic Creme de Cafe $1.25
Signature Creme de Cafe and your choice of Sambuca, Amaretto or Frangelico. $2.45

Cappuccino
Cafe Rich espresso frothed with cream and a hint of chocolate, topped with whipped cream. $1.75
Signature Cappuccino with your choice of Sambuca, Amaretto or Frangelico & topped with whipped cream. $2.95

Old Fashioned Milk Shake
Vanilla, Chocolate, Strawberry $2.25

Soda, Coffee, Specialty & Iced Teas, Sparkling Mineral Waters and Flavored Seltzers... Perrier... Pelegrino... Saratoga... NY Seltzer, Clausthaler Non-Alcoholic Beer
(Unlimited refills of Soda, Coffee, Decaf & Tea)

"Carmella's serves a Full Menu 'til Midnight!"

AMERICAN · ITALIAN FARE

"All menu available for just ask for

TEASERS

Garlic Pizza
A basket of hot, tender, crispy wedges. $3.25

Buffalo-Style Chicken Wings
A large order of spicy chicken wings served with celery sticks and cool bleu cheese dressing. $4.65

Chicken Tenderloins
Breaded, fried tender and served with bar-b-que and horseradish sauce. $4.45

Onion Rings
A generous basket of sweet, whole rings, dipped in beer batter and fried crisp. $2.45

Toasted Ravioli
Lightly breaded pasta pillows stuffed with cheese and fried to a golden brown and served with our special marinara sauce. $3.45

Mushroom Fritters
Fresh mushrooms, batter-dipped and fried, served with cherry mustard sauce for dipping. $3.95

Pizza Fried Dough
Fresh fried dough served with your choice of butter and sugar, cinnamon sugar, garlic and oil, or marinara sauce for dipping. $2.75

Fresh Cut Fries
Homemade, Hot & Crispy! (Please let us know if they're not!)
Large basket $1.65   With cheese sauce $.95 extra

Fried Mozzarella
Crisp, golden mozzarella with a soft, creamy center served with marinara sauce for dipping. $4.75   "Homemade"

Fried Zucchini
Fresh zucchini sticks rolled through seasoned bread crumbs and dusted with fresh romano. Served with tartar sauce. $3.45

Loaded Potato Skins
Potato skins fried until golden. Loaded with cheddar cheese and bacon. Served with sour cream. $6.45
Half orders available upon request $4.25

Jumbo Shrimp Cocktail
Imported, plump and tender. $5.95

Nacho Mamma's

RESTAURANT/OPERATOR
Nacho Mamma's
Des Moines, IA
YEAR OPENED
1991
DESIGN FIRM
Sayles Graphic Design
DESIGNER
John Sayles
PRINTER
Printing Station
MATERIAL
Chipboard

Nacho Mamma's is located in a space previously occupied by another Mexican restaurant. The client wanted its own unique visual identity, something that would allow people to realize that more was offered than typical Mexican fare. The design firm's participation grew to include menu design and advertising as well as interior and exterior graphics. John Sayles, principal of Sayles Graphic Design said, "My involvement in the visual identity of Nacho Mamma's has been a designer's dream. The owners were willing to take the time to help me to understand the restaurant business, and I was glad to help them understand my field as well. The result is a wonderful blend of what works and what looks good." Nacho Mamma's management involved Mr. Sayles in the restaurant's interior and exterior design as well. The project blends extremely well and gives the restaurant a single, cohesive look. Future plans include retail packaging for such products as salsa and tortillas. These will utilize the restaurant's already established visual identity.

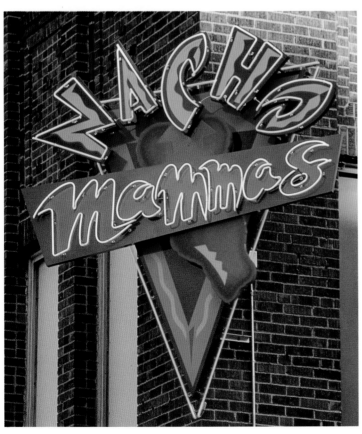

CHAPTER
6
Ethnic Menus

China Coast Bamboo

RESTAURANT/OPERATOR
China Coast
General Mills Restaurants, Inc.
Orlando, FL
YEAR OPENED
1990
DESIGN FIRM
Robinson's, Inc.
DESIGNER
Blaine Sweatt
ART DIRECTOR
Valerie Clelland
PRINTER
Robinson's, Inc.

This menu was designed to help customers and employees better understand the differences in China's many regional cooking styles. It serves as a guide to help simplify the nature of Chinese food. The cover design, an ink wash painting of bamboo, is highlighted by Chinese characters. The bamboo theme is repeated throughout the restaurant by interior and exterior plantings. Inside the menu, three maps,

each on a separate page, highlight the different regions of China. Explanatory copy notes the ingredients indigenous to each region's cooking. The maps are echoed by a similar large canvas relief of China that hangs in the lobby.

This menu won the "Grand Prize" in the 1991 Great Menu Contest sponsored by the NRA. It also won a First Place in the "Average Check $8-$15" category.

Duwamps Cafe Late Menu

RESTAURANT/OPERATOR
Duwamps Cafe,
Seattle Brewing Company
Seattle, WA
DESIGN FIRM
Tim Girvin Design, Inc.
DESIGNER
Stephen Pannone
ART DIRECTOR
Tim Girvin
ILLUSTRATOR
Tim Girvin

Duwamps is the Native American word for Seattle. The crow, prominently featured on the restaurant's menu, is related to local Indian lore. It is two-color printed on a parchment-like paper with a high contrast black foil-stamp.

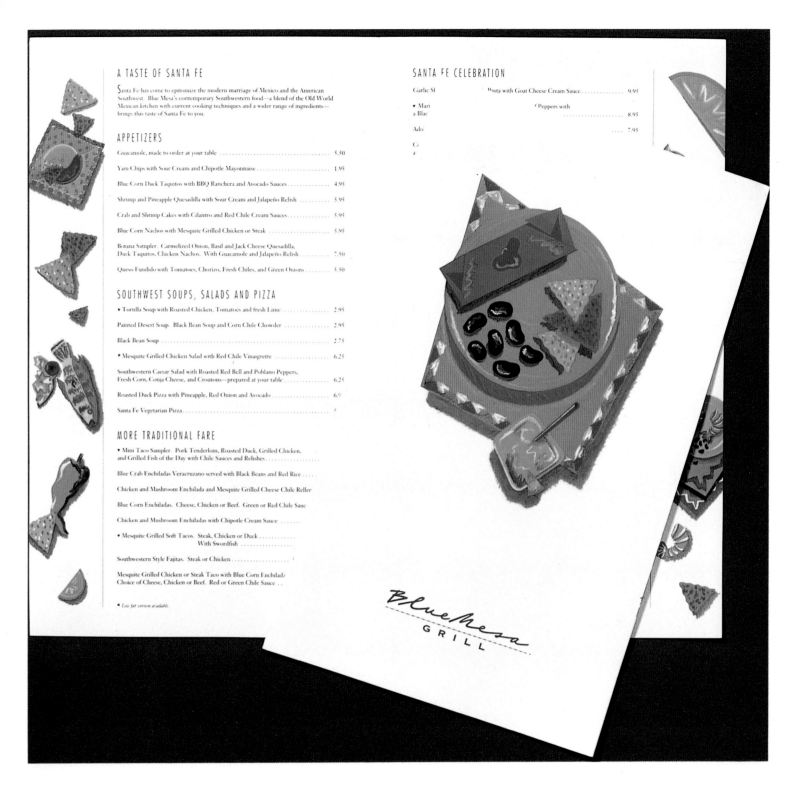

A TASTE OF SANTA FE

Santa Fe has come to epitomize the modern marriage of Mexico and the American Southwest. Blue Mesa's contemporary Southwestern food—a blend of the Old World Mexican kitchen with current cooking techniques and a wider range of ingredients—brings this taste of Santa Fe to you.

APPETIZERS

Guacamole, made to order at your table	5.50
Yam Chips with Sour Cream and Chipotle Mayonnaise	1.95
Blue Corn Duck Taquitos with BBQ Ranchera and Avocado Sauces	4.95
Shrimp and Pineapple Quesadilla with Sour Cream and Jalapeño Relish	5.95
Crab and Shrimp Cakes with Cilantro and Red Chile Cream Sauces	5.95
Blue Corn Nachos with Mesquite Grilled Chicken or Steak	5.95
Botana Sampler. Carmelized Onion, Basil and Jack Cheese Quesadilla, Duck Taquitos, Chicken Nachos. With Guacamole and Jalapeño Relish	7.50
Queso Fundido with Tomatoes, Chorizo, Fresh Chiles, and Green Onions	5.50

SOUTHWEST SOUPS, SALADS AND PIZZA

♥ Tortilla Soup with Roasted Chicken, Tomatoes and fresh Lime	2.95
Painted Desert Soup. Black Bean Soup and Corn Chile Chowder	2.95
Black Bean Soup	2.75
♥ Mesquite Grilled Chicken Salad with Red Chile Vinaigrette	6.25
Southwestern Caesar Salad with Roasted Red Bell and Poblano Peppers, Fresh Corn, Cotija Cheese, and Croutons—prepared at your table	6.25
Roasted Duck Pizza with Pineapple, Red Onion and Avocado	6.9
Santa Fe Vegetarian Pizza	?

MORE TRADITIONAL FARE

♥ Mini Taco Sampler. Pork Tenderloin, Roasted Duck, Grilled Chicken, and Grilled Fish of the Day with Chile Sauces and Relishes	
Blue Crab Enchiladas Veracruzano served with Black Beans and Red Rice	
Chicken and Mushroom Enchilada and Mesquite Grilled Cheese Chile Reller	
Blue Corn Enchiladas. Cheese, Chicken or Beef. Green or Red Chile Sauce	
Chicken and Mushroom Enchiladas with Chipotle Cream Sauce	
♥ Mesquite Grilled Soft Tacos. Steak, Chicken or Duck	
With Swordfish	
Southwestern Style Fajitas. Steak or Chicken	
Mesquite Grilled Chicken or Steak Taco with Blue Corn Enchilada Choice of Cheese, Chicken or Beef. Red or Green Chile Sauce	

♥ Low fat version available.

SANTA FE CELEBRATION

Garlic Sl	Pasta with Goat Cheese Cream Sauce	9.95
♥ Mari a Blac	Peppers with	8.95
Ado		7.95
G a		

Blue Mesa GRILL

Blue Mesa Grill

RESTAURANT/OPERATOR
Blue Mesa Grill/deNada Restaurants Dallas, TX
YEAR OPENED
1988
DESIGN FIRM
Benoit Design, Inc.
DESIGNER
Tracy Russell
ART DIRECTOR
Dennis Benoit
ILLUSTRATOR
Debbie Allen
PRINTER
John's Printing

The Blue Mesa Grill is a Santa Fe-style restaurant serving contemporary Southwestern fare. The unique food, with drinks like the blue marguerita, the Southwestern art, and even the wait staff attired in turquoise shirts and bolo ties, work to create a true Santa Fe style.

The menu was successful in representing the restaurant as a contemporary and colorful Southwestern grill.

Blue Mesa Grill was a 1992 NRA winner in two categories. It won a First Place for restaurants with an "Average Check between $8-$15" and was a Second Place Grand Prize winner.

Inn of the Anasazi Menu Series

RESTAURANT/OPERATOR
The Restaurant—Inn of the Anasazi/
Robert D. Zimmer Group
Santa Fe, NM
YEAR OPENED
1991
DESIGN FIRM
David Carter Graphic Design
DESIGNER
Lori Wilson
PRINTER
Etheridge

This small rustic inn, located in
Santa Fe, is adorned with natural
fabrics and native pottery that give the
texture and flavor of the surrounding
area. In keeping with this concept, the
entire graphics program was designed
with recycled papers and materials with
textural qualities that reflect the
restaurant's location. The menu cover
is cloth bound and recreates the
authentic pictographic cave paintings
left behind by the Anasazi Indians.

Stoyanof's

RESTAURANT/OPERATOR
Stoyanof, Inc.
San Francisco, CA
DESIGN FIRM
Warren Welter Design
DESIGNER/ILLUSTRATOR
Warren Welter
PRINTER
Great Impressions
PAPER
Speckletone

Stoyanof's, a restaurant serving Greek cuisine, wanted a nontraditional menu design for its second location in San Francisco. The goal was to create a colorful collection of menus and yet remain cost effective. The solution was a series of four different illustrations that were printed on six colors of Speckletone paper. Through creative ink and paper combinations, a total of 24 different color combinations were produced. Using woodcut style illustrations and a tranquil color palette, the simple charm of Greek village cooking is captured in a contemporary fashion.

la Cité

RESTAURANT/OPERATOR
la Cité
The New York Restaurant Group, Inc.
New York, NY
YEAR OPENED
1990
DESIGN FIRM
Rossin Studios
DESIGNER
Linda Rossin
PRINTER
Applied Graphics

La Cité wanted a menu cover that used
the logo to make a strong statement.
Made of coated paper it holds a
parchment insert in a cleverly disguised
pocket.

Zuni Grill

RESTAURANT/OPERATOR
Zuni Grill
West Coast Restaurant Ventures
Irvine, CA
YEAR OPENED
1991
DESIGN FIRM
On The Edge
DESIGNER
Jeff Gasper
ART DIRECTOR
Karyn Verdak
ILLUSTRATORS
Joe Mozdzen/Karyn Verdak
PRINTER
Sand Graphics

The Zuni Grill is a warm, inviting
authentic Indian cave recreated in
Hollywood style via three-dimensional
cave walls, icon-decorated tabletops,
contemporary Indian art and with an
up-to-the-minute exhibition kitchen.
Lighting design was given a high
priority. The restaurant combines the
award-winning Southwestern cuisine of
David Wilhelm, with the drama of a
movie set. The Zuni Grill's powerful
concept gives this shopping center-
based restaurant, a distinct advantage
over the usual mall fare.

The menu originated as a three-
dimensional, hand-painted plaster
sculpture. Painted in layers it was then
topped off with a logo and supporting
icon images. Photographed by candle-
light to truly capture the dramatic feel,
the image was then used for the
menu's cover. The inside pages are
updated weekly by the restaurant using
a Macintosh computer.

Golden Temple

RESTAURANT/OPERATOR
Golden Temple
Brookline, MA
YEAR OPENED
1970, renovated in 1989
DESIGN FIRM
Monica Banks and Co.
DESIGNER
Monica Banks
ILLUSTRATOR
Monica Banks
PRINTER
Pride Printers

The designer procured Chinese foods including a smallmouth bass, bok choy, orange segments, mushroom caps and even chicken feet, and used them to print the graphics. This technique follows the ancient Chinese art of fish printing. The designer combined the different elements to create mutant fish characters all with the same facial expression. There are four menus in the series, each with contrasting colored covers printed on a coated paper. The interiors are held in place with elastic string bearing a single gold bead.

The temple-like design of the restaurant is by the architect Ahearn Shopfer.

Cafe Japengo

RESTAURANT/OPERATOR
Cafe Japengo/Hyatt Regency
La Jolla, CA
YEAR OPENED
1990
DESIGN FIRM
David Carter Graphic Design
DESIGNER
Randall Hill
PRINTER
Jarvis Press

Cafe Japengo is a contemporary
Japanese restaurant. Black chairs and
tables with red accents dominate the
interior. Although this menu design
with its swirling brush stroke is ultra
contemporary, it is the essence of
Japanese art and culture.

Bistro 110

RESTAURANT/OPERATOR
Bistro 110/The Levy Organization
Chicago, IL
YEAR OPENED
1984
DESIGN FIRM
The Levy Organization—in house
creative services
DESIGNER
Marcy Lansing
ILLUSTRATORS
Menu illustrator: Marcy Lansing
4-color art illustration: Judy Rifka
PRINTER
Printing Arts, Inc.

In the great European tradition, Bistro 110 is an informal neighborhood restaurant for locals and Chicago visitors alike. The look is warm and welcoming with the restaurant's simple, unpretentious interior serving as the inspiration for menu graphics. The loose, airy drawings on the cover convey the restaurant's light, comfortable atmosphere and fulfill the client's desire for a functional menu. Printed in-house on a weekly basis, menu shells containing the headings and the brightly printed cover are capable of going through the restaurant's photocopier.

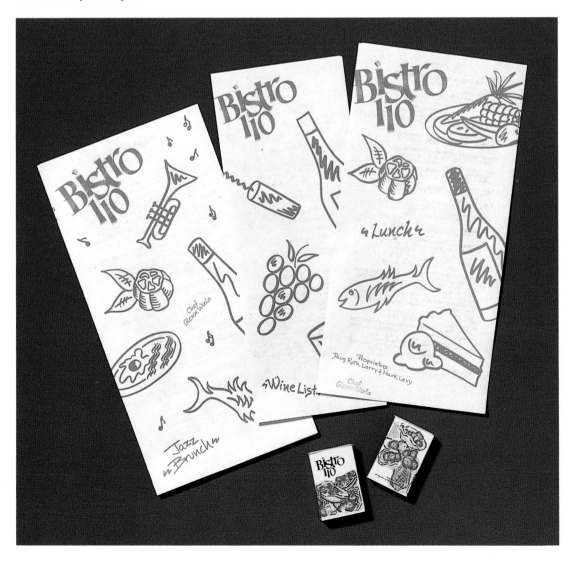

Restaurant Petrus

RESTAURANT/OPERATOR
Restaurant Petrus
Island Shangri-La
Hong Kong, Hong Kong
YEAR OPENED
1990
DESIGN FIRM
David Carter Graphic Design
DESIGNER
Waitak Lai
PRINTER
Goodwill Printing, Hong Kong

The name Petrus was derived from a small vineyard in France that produced a wine of some renown, bearing the same name. Although the overall interior scheme of this hotel is a blending of Eastern and Western elements, its premiere restaurant is exclusively French. The designer's challenge was to create an upscale menu series for the downtown Hong Kong restaurant that could meld the two varying concepts. The designer selected French paintings with painstaking detail that coordinate with the restaurant's interior.

Croc's, Boca Raton

RESTAURANT/OPERATOR
Croc's, Boca Raton/Willmax, Inc.
Boca Raton, FL
DESIGN FIRM
David Savage/Art & Design
DESIGNER
David Savage
ILLUSTRATOR
David Savage
PRINTER
Point to Point Graphics

Croc's, with the casual atmosphere of a Caribbean island celebration and Boca Raton style and sophistication, is anything but boring. It is the kind of place where an eight-foot crocodile carved out of solid mahogany somehow seems to fit with a real two-seat helicopter. With sixteen-foot high ceilings, the open and airy room is a nice blend of old weathered signs that

evoke remote island fantasies. An endless array of carefully chosen paraphernalia serves as a casual, but comfortable backdrop for patrons dressed in everything from three-piece suits to Bermuda shorts.

The graphic image contributes to the casual island theme set by the restaurant's decor. The colorful logo, in a native, Caribbean style, is stunning against the crisp, white background. Because it is inviting and easy to read, the menu serves as another prop for the restaurant theme. Components of the design package include stationery, postcards, T-shirts, and even a short sleeve shirt.

Taipan

RESTAURANT/OPERATOR
Taipan
Los Angeles, CA
YEAR OPENED
1991
DESIGN FIRM
Beck & Graboski Design Office
DESIGNER
Terry Graboski
ART DIRECTOR
Constance Beck
PRINTER
Kion Printing

The designer's assignment was to create a strong identity for Taipan, a new restaurant located in a downtown Los Angeles office building's food court. Because of its location on the mezzanine level, the logo had to be bold and contemporary. Exterior signage needed to be dynamic and highly visible.

A graphic, 64-foot-long dragon over the entry fascia enlivens the restaurant's exterior. It is painted with high gloss lacquers, with airbrushed gradations, and illuminated by neon. The restaurant's simple black-and-white interior is accented by the bright colors of the menu covers. The logo also appears on the podium and on a portable directional sign, as well as on all printed matter. The press sheet shows how the computer-generated skewed gradations of solid PMS colors appear. Each menu is laminated and the interior printed in a contrasting solid double black.

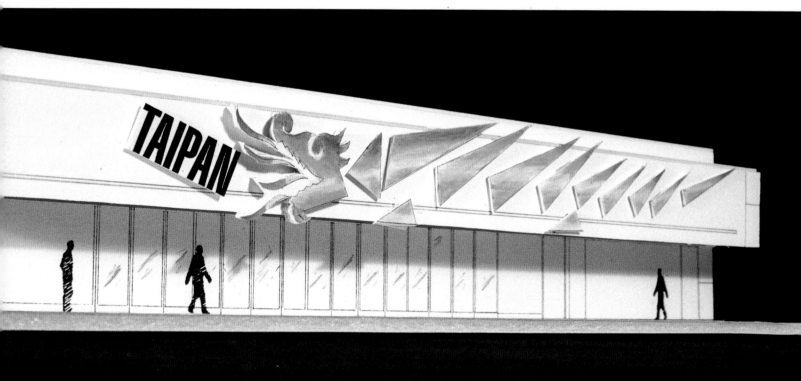

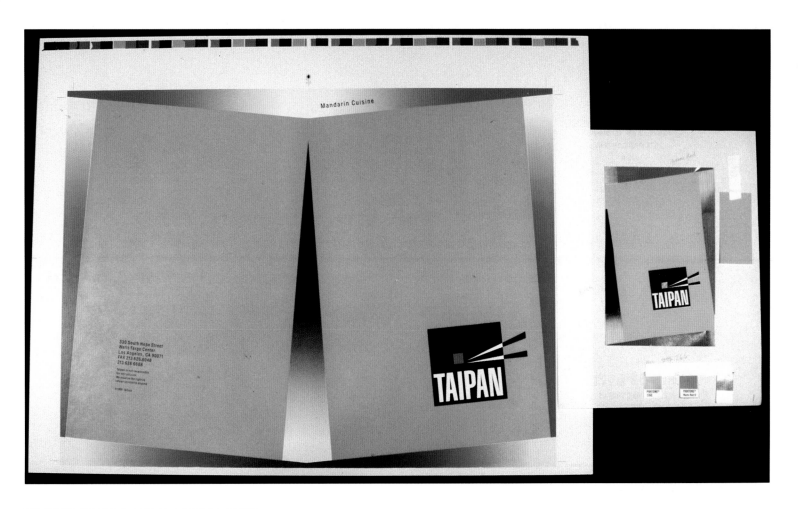

CHAPTER

7

By Air,
By Land,
By Sea

British Airways

RESTAURANT/OPERATOR
British Airways
Jackson Heights, NY
DESIGN FIRM
David Davies Associates

British Airways Club Class cuisine was introduced in January 1988. It was part of an award-winning introduction to business class on trans-Atlantic flights. British Airways prides itself on style and comfort, and for providing the right ambience to appeal to this upscale market. The design concept included cabin interiors, as well as food service and food presentation. The contoured seats and coordinated interior design of the Club Class cabin create a luxurious atmosphere for in-flight dining.

The menu is a minimalist design featuring the company's corporate blue and gray colors. The appealing use of color and typeface have made this design as appropriate in 1992 as it was when it was first introduced.

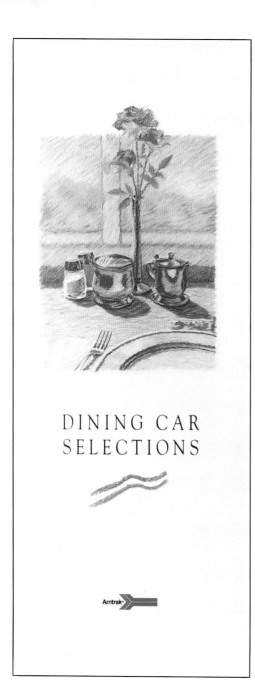

DINING CAR
SELECTIONS

~~

Amtrak➤

Amtrak Dining Car and First Class

RESTAURANT/OPERATOR
Amtrak
Washington, DC
DESIGN FIRM
E. James White, Co.
DESIGNER
Tom Sadowski
ILLUSTRATORS
Larry Fickau and Nathan Davies

The first class dining menus, befitting the upscale traveler, needed to be elegant and sophisticated. These menus are given to dining car patrons by on-board attendants during breakfast, lunch and dinner. They work well with the china used on many of Amtrak's long distance trains.

These large, placemat style wall menus are displayed in cafe cars aboard Amtrak trains. There are two distinct versions, one targeted to business people and the other catering primarily to leisure travelers. The rationale behind these new menus was to have something striking, something that would give the dining car a fresh look. The designer chose an Art Deco style as a tribute to the golden age of rail travel. The client specified that the menus needed to be inviting, but more importantly, in an effort to generate food sales, they had to be readable to the casual passerby. In addition, the chosen color scheme had to complement the already existing interior.

Amtrak➤

SANDWICHES

HOT BREAKFAST SANDWICH 2.50 *Egg, Smoked Ham and Cheese*	**TUNA SALAD** 3.50 *on Stone Ground Whole Wheat*
GOURMET CHICKEN SALAD 3.75 *on a Croissant*	**TODAY'S FEATURED LIGHT CREAM CHEESE SANDWICH** 2.75
HAM AND SWISS CHEESE 3.50 *on Rye*	**LARGE ALL BEEF HOT DOG** 2.25
SPECIALTY CHICKEN BREAST 3.75 *on a Soft Hoagie Roll*	

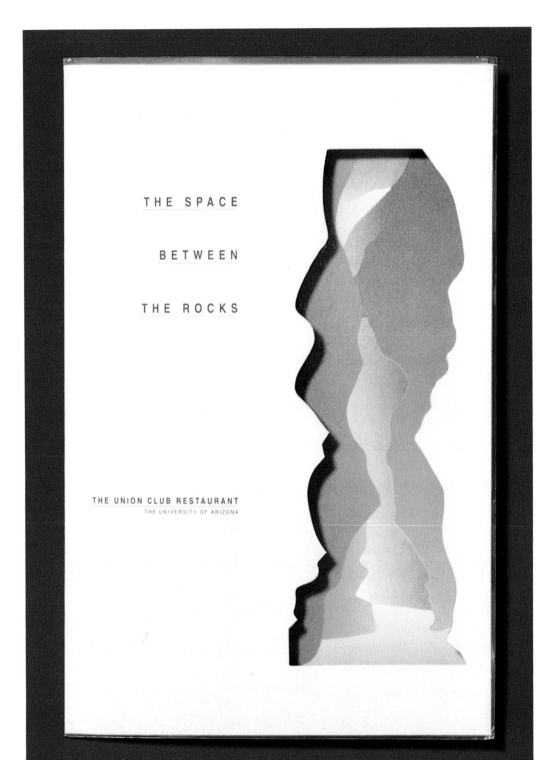

The Space Between The Rocks

RESTAURANT/OPERATOR
Union Club Restaurant
Tucson, AZ
YEAR OPENED
1971
DESIGN FIRM
University of Arizona
Student Union Dining Services
DESIGNER
Erin Feeney
PHOTOGRAPHER
Dana Slaymaker
PRINTER
Owl Printing

Each year students at the University of Arizona create a new menu design and restaurant concept for the student union's Union Club. The theme is always designed around something that reflects the State of Arizona. This design features the surreal beauty of its slot canyons, a common feature in the state. A total of 21, 30-inch square cibachromes by Dana Slaymaker of these canyons are featured. The objective was to give patrons the feeling of what it would be like to be standing in a slot canyon. As you enter the restaurant, there is a life size 84-inch tall image to give the impact of an actual slot canyon.

With the cover design, viewers get a better feeling for the Southwestern environment. Earth-toned recycled paper, reminiscent of sand, was chosen to reflect the desert; a die-cut gives it a windowed effect. The menu's interior features a computer-generated image in tones of blue and gold. These same shades are prominent in the large photograph at the restaurant's entry. Also included is a short explanatory note written by Ms. Slaymaker.

The Union Club Restaurant was a 1992 NRA Second Place winner in the "Institutional" category.

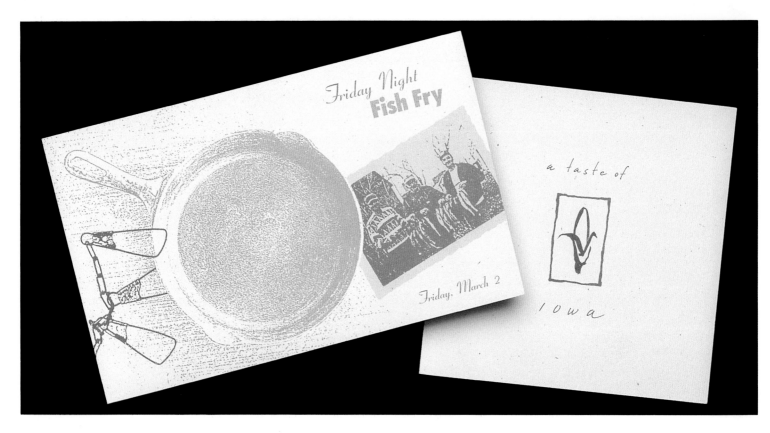

A Taste of Iowa and Fish Fry

RESTAURANT/OPERATOR
**Iowa State University—
Residence Department Food Service
Ames, IA**
YEAR OPENED
1865
DESIGN FIRM
Iowa State University Students
DESIGNER
Franke Design

Iowa State University's Residence
Department Food Service hosts a series
of bi-weekly special events throughout
the school year. For each of these
events, a special menu is designed and
produced by the ISU graphic arts
students. "A Taste of Iowa" won
Second Place in the 1991 NRA Great
Menu Contest Award in the
"Institutional Food Service" category.

Special Events Planner and Royal Weddings

RESTAURANT/OPERATOR
**Hotel Queen Mary
Long Beach, CA**
DESIGN FIRM
Kenyon Press
ART DIRECTOR
Richard Witt
ILLUSTRATORS
**Richard Witt (Royal Weddings);
Robert Greisen (Special Events)**
PRINTER
Kenyon Press

Designed to house several different
elements, this special events planner is
a small capacity folder featuring two
die-cut pockets. The Art Deco design is
a hallmark of the Queen Mary. In the
case of the "royal weddings"
brochure, the characteristic illustration
and background were tabled. In its
place, a framed oval photo of the
"shop of dreams" and a wedding lace
background fashioned via gloss and
dull varnish were used.

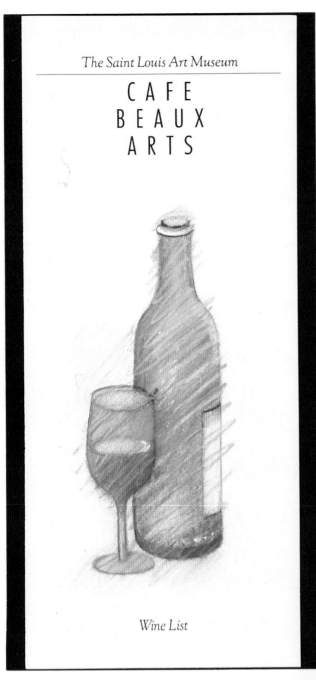

The Saint Louis Art Museum

CAFE
BEAUX
ARTS

Wine List

Art Museum's Cafe Beaux Arts
Wine List

RESTAURANT/OPERATOR
Cafe Beaux Arts
The Saint Louis Art Museum
St. Louis, MO
YEAR OPENED
1985
DESIGN FIRM
Heller Rosenfeld Design
DESIGNER
Julie Rosenfeld
ILLUSTRATOR
Julie Rosenfeld
PRINTER
Dale Printing Company

Located in the Saint Louis Art
Museum, Cafe Beaux Art's wine list
was created to be a work of art. It
needed to be simple yet elegant to
harmonize with the restrained but
warm interior of the cafe.

Air Canada

RESTAURANT/OPERATOR
Air Canada In-Flight Service
Montreal Quebec, Canada
YEAR OPENED
1937
DESIGN FIRM
Morris Graphics
DESIGNER
M. Moran
PRINTER
Morris Graphics

Air Canada chose to salute "Grand
Openings of the World" for its first
class menu series by using brilliant
color photographs of famous doors,
windows and gates. The door featured
is from Beethoven's birthplace in
Bonn, Germany. The stained glass
window is from the House of
Commons in Ottawa, Ontario and the
gate is at Buckingham Palace in
London.

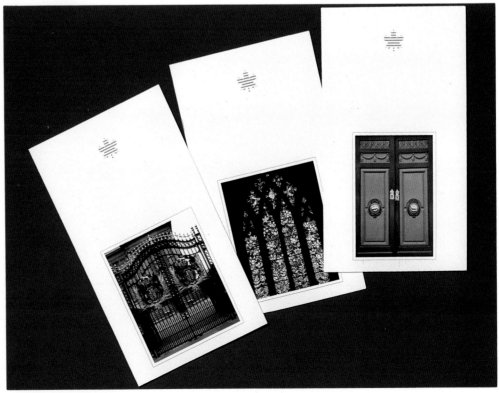

International Flagship Service

RESTAURANT/OPERATOR
American Airlines
Fort Worth, TX
DESIGN FIRM
Bozell Dallas
DESIGNER
Lorraine Kuehnel
ILLUSTRATOR
Kelly Stribling
PRINTER
O'Sullivan Menus

These handsomely illustrated menus are used for American Airlines international service for both first and business classes. The renderings of food were used to convey the quality and attention to detail the airline gives to the meals served aboard its flights. The client wanted something that would let the traveler know these were not going to be the usual in-flight meals that air passengers have grown used to. The menus are printed in both English and German. What makes the wine list particularly interesting is the historic reference and in-depth explanation given for each offering.

American Flagship Service

RESTAURANT/OPERATOR
American Airlines
Fort Worth, TX
DESIGN FIRM
Swid Powell
DESIGNER
Smatt Florence, Inc.
PRINTER
O'Sullivan Menus

When flying between New York and Los Angeles on American Airlines these menus are presented to each traveler. The cover, with its famous view of the Hollywood Hills seen through a stand of tall palm trees, was done in dark shades of blue and gray.

RESTAURANT/OPERATOR
Mount Carmel East Hospital
Birthing Center
Columbus, OH
YEAR OPENED
1990
DESIGN FIRM
Mt. Carmel East Creative Services
ART DIRECTOR
Nutritional Services Department
PRINTER
Fine Line Graphics

Mount Carmel East Hospital Birthing Center in Columbus, Ohio, provides a special celebratory menu. It is tailored to new parents just before they go home with their new baby. The client wanted something that would complement the facilities' decor. So the menu needed a special look, something that was adaptable to patients with special needs and that would still work within the hospital's existing systems. Printed on recycled paper, two of its pages are perforated, one for "mom" the other for "guests." They both feature healthy foods that can be selected by using the check-off system common to most hospitals.

These menus took Third Place in the 1991 NRA Great Menu Contest in the "Institutional Food Service" category.

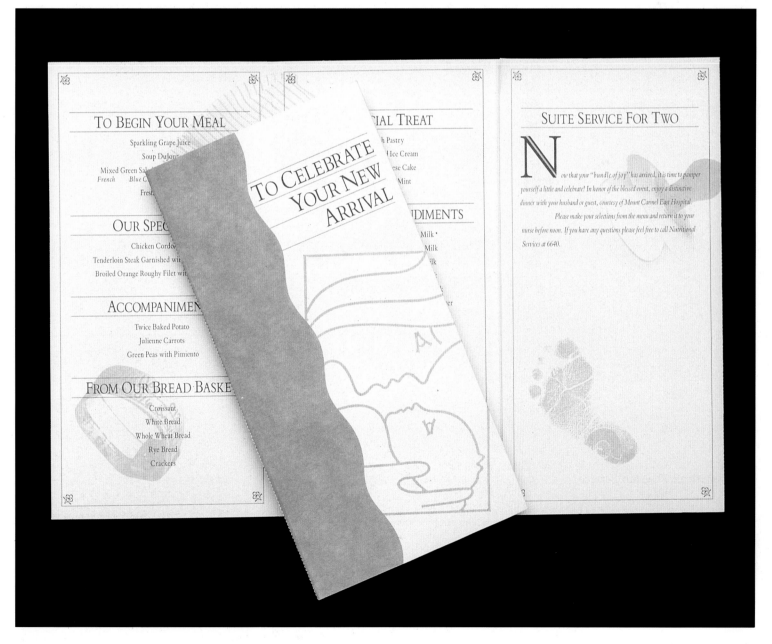

CHAPTER
8

All
Shapes
and Sizes

Beaches & Cream

RESTAURANT/OPERATOR
Beaches & Cream
Disney Development Co.
Lake Buena Vista, FL
YEAR OPENED
1990
DESIGN FIRM
David Carter Graphic Design
DESIGNER
Lori Wilson
ILLUSTRATORS
Lori Wilson and Kevin Prejean

Beaches & Cream is an old-fashioned
ice cream parlor and soda fountain at
Disney's Beach Club in Orlando,
Florida. The fun-filled decor is done in
pastels with striped beach balls, white
wrought iron parlor tables and chairs,
and a turn-of-the-century soda
fountain. Employees are attired in
period costumes.

Luau Masks

RESTAURANT/OPERATOR
**Grand Hyatt Wailea
Maui, HI**
DESIGN FIRM
Associates
DESIGNER
Donna Milord
ILLUSTRATOR
Bobbie Warehan
PRINTER
Associates

The first Hawaiians traveled thousands of miles from distant lands to inhabit this island paradise. As this menu tells us in its brief text, "the cargo they cherished most was the food that they cultivated to sustain life. Glorious thanksgiving celebrations of dancing, fun, games, and much eating began with a thankful prayer to the God Lono for his blessings of an abundant land and sea." The Grand Hyatt Wailea's Luau honors the ancient god and reflects the spirit and pageantry of old Hawaii. This series of three luau mask menus were recreated using pencil illustrations on thin wood. They are then reproduced and presented to guests as souvenirs.

The menu shown displays:

ORTS OF CALL

ARI SAPPHIRE
phire and Absolute Citron.
Harry's Own
6.50

H ALA COPA
of Tropical Juices
ribbean Rums
6.50

'S TWISTER
ich Vanilla Ice Cream
Creme de Menthe
ur Bobby Sox Off!
6.50

IA COOLER
Melon Colada
with Midori
6.50

Lobby Lounge

Lobby Lounge,
Walt Disney World
Dolphin Hotel

RESTAURANT/OPERATOR
Lobby Lounge
Walt Disney World Dolphin Hotel
Orlando, FL
YEAR OPENED
1990
DESIGN FIRM
Kenyon Press
DESIGNER
Richard Witt
ILLUSTRATOR
Richard Witt
PRINTER
Kenyon Press

One of the many pieces designed for the opening of Orlando's Walt Disney World Dolphin Hotel, this menu was developed through communication with Michael Graves, the hotel's architect and interior designer. The palm frond motif is repeated throughout the atrium-style lounge, but is most notably found in an exotic wall mural. It seemed only natural to use it again for the tabletop menu as well. Both the cover and a four-page insert were die-cut, then stitched and folded to make the menu self-standing.

SUMMERTIME LUNCH SPECIALS
(11:00 a.m. – 3:00 p.m.)

MORE MULBERRY STREET SPECIALS
(All lunch size pastas below include a freshly baked garlic homeloaf.
Soup or Salad with any Mulberry Special, add $1.95)

RIGATONI WITH MUSHROOM SAUCE   4.95
Fresh button mushrooms sautéed with garlic and East Side's own zesty
tomato sauce and served over rigatoni noodles.

LINGUINE WITH CLAM SAUCE   5.95
A pasta specialty from New York's "Little Italy" – clams, garlic and Italian
herbs in a plum tomato sauce served over linguine.

CHICKEN TETTRAZINI   5.95
Chicken breast sautéed with mushrooms, garlic, fresh chopped tomatoes,
cream and parmesan cheese and served over linguine noodles.

ZUCCHINI CACCIATORE   4.95
Zucchini, red and green peppers simmered with sweet basil, onions and
tomatoes then baked and topped with melted mozzarella cheese.

COOL CANAL STREET SPECIALS
(Add a bowl of Italian vegetable soup for $1.95)

INSALATA DI PASTA   4.95
Fusilli pasta mixed with capicolla, salami, mozzarella cheese, tomatoes,
fresh peppers and East Side's herb vinaigrette.

FRUIT AND VEGGIE PLATE   4.95
Seasonal fresh fruit and cool crisp veggies served with creamy garlic dip.

CHICKEN SALAD PLATE   5.75
Tender chicken breast mixed with celery, green onions and mayo and
served with tomatoes, olives and a hard boiled egg.

CHICKEN SALAD KAISER   4.25
East Side's chunky chicken salad served on a fresh kaiser.
(Add fresh cut fries for $1.95)

EAST SIDE MARIO'S
Cuddy FARMS

An American Italian Eatery

Tsunami

RESTAURANT/OPERATOR
Grand Hyatt Wailea
Maui, HI
DESIGN FIRM
Associates
DESIGNER
Donna Milord
PRINTER
Associates

Tsunami is the Japanese word meaning tidal wave and the name of this multi-million dollar club on the island of Maui. The menu is actually a hand held custom wave machine complete with blue water, starfish and sea shells.

This most unusual menu accommodates a self sticking acetate menu list on the front side.

Tsunami was a 1992 NRA First Place winner in the "Most Imaginative" category.

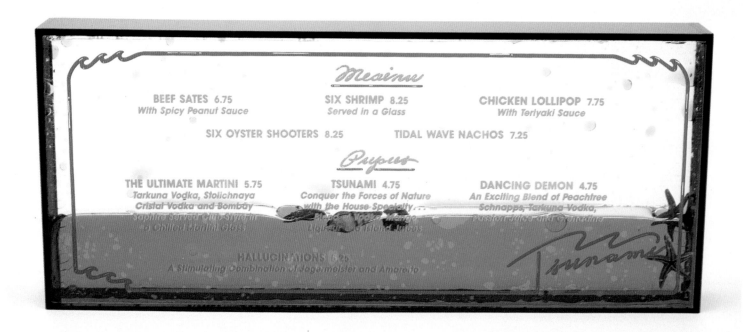

Menu

BEEF SATES 6.75
With Spicy Peanut Sauce

SIX SHRIMP 8.25
Served in a Glass

CHICKEN LOLLIPOP 7.75
With Teriyaki Sauce

SIX OYSTER SHOOTERS 8.25   **TIDAL WAVE NACHOS** 7.25

Pupus

THE ULTIMATE MARTINI 5.75
*Tarkuna Vodka, Stolichnaya
Cristal Vodka and Bombay
Saphire Served Club Style in
a Chilled Martini Glass*

TSUNAMI 4.75
*Conquer the Forces of Nature
with the House Specialty...
Liqueur and Island Juices*

DANCING DEMON 4.75
*An Exciting Blend of Peachtree
Schnapps, Tarkuna Vodka,
Passion Juice and Grenadine*

HALLUCINATIONS 6.25
A Stimulating Combination of Jagermeister and Amaretto

Summertime Lunch Specials

RESTAURANT/OPERATOR
East Side Mario's
Prime Restaurant Group
Mississauga, Ontario, Canada
YEAR OPENED
1988
DESIGN FIRM
Marbury Advertising
Communications
ART DIRECTOR
Heather Gentleman
ILLUSTRATOR
Jodie Rock
PRINTER
Spirit Graphics
PAPER
laminated

East Side Mario's uses a giant red tomato-shaped menu to introduce special summertime lunch items in eye-catching fashion. The inspiration for the unusual shape of this menu came from the giant tomato over the restaurant's exterior entrance. It also serves to underscore the eatery's Italian theme as well.

Concrete Daiquiri

RESTAURANT/OPERATOR
Tony Roma's
Dallas, TX
YEAR OPENED
1970
DESIGN FIRM
Baker & Grooms
DESIGNERS
Mikie Baker and Lindy Grooms
ILLUSTRATOR
Dave Kramer
PRINTER
Allcraft

The construction theme of this daiquiri menu grew out of the renovation Tony Roma's was undergoing. The restaurant wanted to promote this special drink during the transitional period. This table tent transformed the construction environment into a kind of temporary decor and provided a positive sales message.

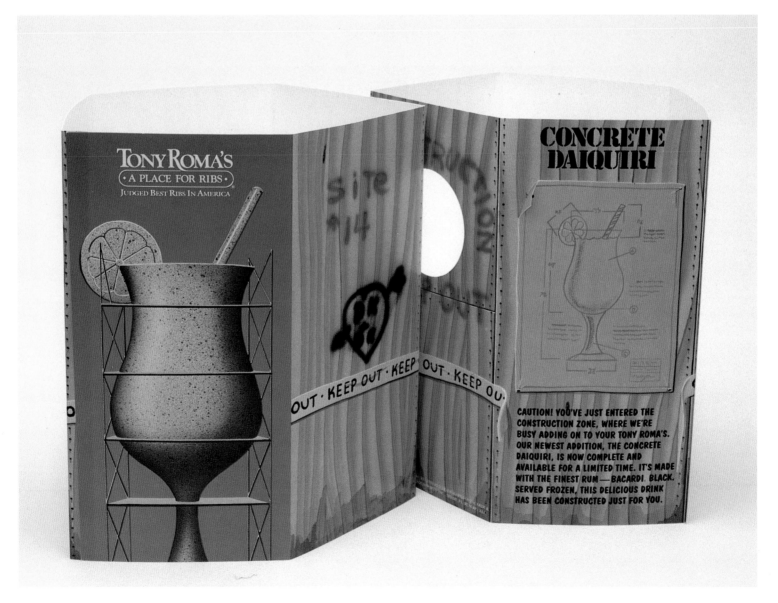

Braille Menu

RESTAURANT/OPERATOR
Loews Anatole Hotel
Dallas, TX
DESIGN FIRM
In House

The Loews Anatole Hotel in Dallas took extra steps to make certain that guests from the national meeting of the President's Committee on Employment of People with Disabilities (PCEPD) were satisfied with the service. Over 2,000 disabled men and women attended the convention. The hotel's convention services worked closely with the PCEPD meeting planner to determine what could be done to accommodate each attendee. One of their suggestions was that the hotel offer braille menus in selected restaurants and at the front desk. The hotel contacted a local organization that services the needs of visually impaired individuals and had them convert their menus and guest services directory into braille. The resulting menu is functional as well as readable and easy to handle. They have been available since May 1991 and are still in use in each of the hotel's restaurants.

The Office

RESTAURANT/OPERATOR
The Office/Restaurant Associates
New York, NY
DESIGN FIRM
The Menu Design Group, Inc.
DESIGNER
W. Scott Mahr
ILLUSTRATOR
Greg Fitzhugh

What would better suit a restaurant with a name like The Office than a menu cover that looks like an attaché case. By using familiar motifs associated with office work, high-lighting items and noting special selections office style, the menu carries the theme both inside and out. Air-brush illustrator, Greg Fitzhugh created a realistic airbrush image that on a quick glance can fool the eye into thinking the menu is actually a brief-case. It has a practical side to it as well, allowing the master artwork to accommodate a one-color, changing text that can be imprinted as needed.

The Library
Ramada Renaissance LAX

RESTAURANT/OPERATOR
Ramada Renaissance LAX
Los Angeles, CA
YEAR OPENED
1991
DESIGN FIRM
Kenyon Press
DESIGNER
Mark Allan
COPYWRITER
Mark Hochstatter
PRINTER
Kenyon Press

The opening of the Ramada Renaissance Los Angeles Airport Hotel, the chain's flagship, proved to be a formidable experience. At the outset, the designers were provided with only a logo and an artist's rendering of the restaurant. The name, The Library, had already been chosen. Given this information, the choice of a book format for menu presentation seemed natural. The original concept consisted of a candy box construction with loose sheets that could be dropped into place. A later modification transformed the design to the present concealed screw-post construction. A library-style pocket was added on the inside left cover to accommodate inserts and highlight specials. The idea to have a bookmark serve as the mini-menu was hit upon during a brain-storming session with the hotel's food and beverage director. Final touches include a permanent tassel for the menu's main reference and a series of four plates, each a portrait of a Renaissance artist. Each portrait is accompanied by a brief biographical sketch of the painter or sculptor. They serve to underscore the association of the word "Renaissance" in the hotel's name.

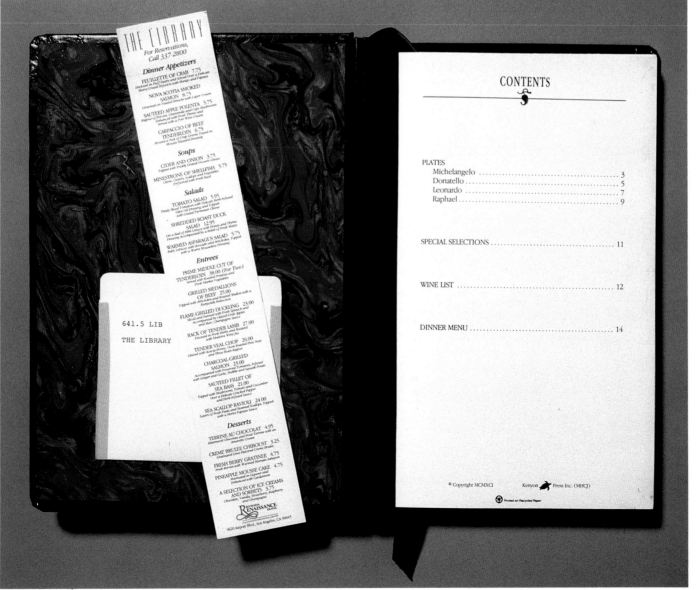

Ellington's Room Service

RESTAURANT/OPERATOR
Ellington's/Embassy Suites Hotel
Indianapolis, IN
DESIGN FIRM
GMI
DESIGNERS
Julie Parmerlee and
Barbara Schwindt
PRINTER
GMI

Most room service menus are heavy leather bound books kept hidden in a drawer. The triangular design of this menu allows it to stand up beside a telephone or on top of the TV in one of the hotel's guest rooms. Using brightly colored graphics, it helps to sell the product in a simple, yet effective manner. By being out in the open, the problem of how to entice people to order from room service has been solved. This menu stands proudly upright, with the phone number displayed on each page.

Ellington's was a 1991 NRA Winner in two categories. It won a "Grand Prize" Second Place and a First Place in the "Specialty" category.

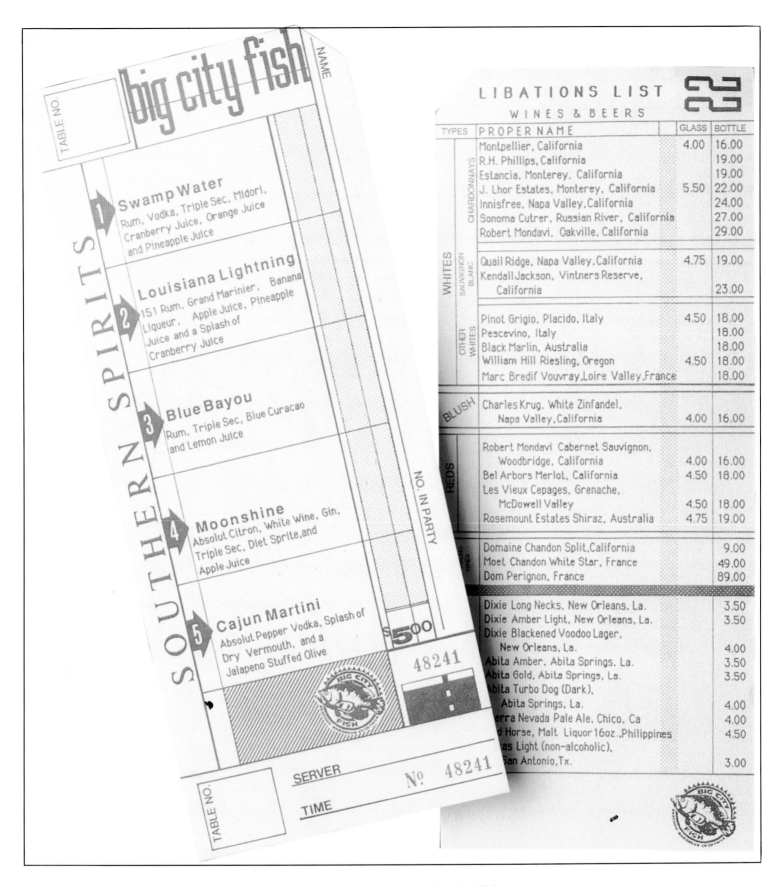

big city fish

NAME

TABLE NO.

SOUTHERN SPIRITS

1 Swamp Water
Rum, Vodka, Triple Sec, Midori,
Cranberry Juice, Orange Juice
and Pineapple Juice

2 Louisiana Lightning
151 Rum, Grand Marinier, Banana
Liqueur, Apple Juice, Pineapple
Juice and a Splash of
Cranberry Juice

3 Blue Bayou
Rum, Triple Sec, Blue Curacao
and Lemon Juice

4 Moonshine
Absolut Citron, White Wine, Gin,
Triple Sec, Diet Sprite, and
Apple Juice

5 Cajun Martini
Absolut Pepper Vodka, Splash of
Dry Vermouth, and a
Jalapeno Stuffed Olive

NO. IN PARTY

$5.00

48241

SERVER   N° 48241

TABLE NO.

TIME

LIBATIONS LIST
WINES & BEERS

TYPES	PROPER NAME	GLASS	BOTTLE
CHARDONNAYS	Montpellier, California	4.00	16.00
	R.H. Phillips, California		19.00
	Estancia, Monterey, California		19.00
	J. Lhor Estates, Monterey, California	5.50	22.00
	Innisfree, Napa Valley, California		24.00
	Sonoma Cutrer, Russian River, California		27.00
	Robert Mondavi, Oakville, California		29.00
SAUVIGNON BLANC	Quail Ridge, Napa Valley, California	4.75	19.00
	Kendall Jackson, Vintners Reserve, California		23.00
OTHER WHITES	Pinot Grigio, Placido, Italy	4.50	18.00
	Pescevino, Italy		18.00
	Black Marlin, Australia		18.00
	William Hill Riesling, Oregon	4.50	18.00
	Marc Bredif Vouvray, Loire Valley, France		18.00
BLUSH	Charles Krug, White Zinfandel, Napa Valley, California	4.00	16.00
REDS	Robert Mondavi Cabernet Sauvignon, Woodbridge, California	4.00	16.00
	Bel Arbors Merlot, California	4.50	18.00
	Les Vieux Cepages, Grenache, McDowell Valley	4.50	18.00
	Rosemount Estates Shiraz, Australia	4.75	19.00
SPARKLING WINES	Domaine Chandon Split, California		9.00
	Moet Chandon White Star, France		49.00
	Dom Perignon, France		89.00
	Dixie Long Necks, New Orleans, La.		3.50
	Dixie Amber Light, New Orleans, La.		3.50
	Dixie Blackened Voodoo Lager, New Orleans, La.		4.00
	Abita Amber, Abita Springs, La.		3.50
	Abita Gold, Abita Springs, La.		3.50
	Abita Turbo Dog (Dark), Abita Springs, La.		4.00
	Sierra Nevada Pale Ale, Chico, Ca		4.00
	Red Horse, Malt Liquor 16oz., Philippines		4.50
	Texas Light (non-alcoholic), San Antonio, Tx.		3.00

WHITES

22

Big City Fish

RESTAURANT/OPERATOR
Big City Fish
Big City Fish Joint Venture
Coconut Grove, FL
YEAR OPENED
1991
DESIGN FIRM
Patrick McBride Company
DESIGNER
Raymond Kampf
ILLUSTRATOR
Raymond Kampf

This drink menu, designed to look like an authentic individually numbered turnpike ticket, coordinates with this restaurant's wacky theme. Lighthearted, but sophisticated, this libations menu fills the bill.

AID & Comfort II American

RESTAURANT/OPERATOR
San Francisco Bay Area restaurants
DESIGN FIRM
Hunt Weber Clark Design
DESIGNER
Nancy Hunt-Weber
ILLUSTRATOR
Julie Wilson
PRINTER
Inky's Printing Establishment

The University of California at Berkeley, along with several well-known Bay Area restaurants and hotels, participated in this one-time fund-raising event to benefit AIDS. There were three separate lunch themes devised, this one with an American accent. The food was donated by a variety of local restaurants including the Fourth Street Grill, Hayes Street Grill and The Fog City Diner. It showed what a group of good-hearted volunteers can do with a little money and a lot of talent.

The components designed consisted of an outer box, which was hand stamped, individually wrapped containers, and even napkins. The menu was a die cut Statue of Liberty.

MENU

Barbecue Chicken
with Lark Creek Barbecue Sauce
HAYES STREET GRILL & LARK CREEK INN

★

Coleslaw with Raspberry Vinaigrette
FOURTH STREET GRILL

★

Pickled Fall Vegetables
HAYES STREET GRILL

★

Cheese Jalapeno Corn Stick
FOG CITY DINER

★

Ginger Cake with Apple Sauce
FOG CITY DINER

Top Draft Picks

RESTAURANT/OPERATOR
Kenyon Press
DESIGN FIRM
Kenyon Press
DESIGNER
Jonathan Wu
ILLUSTRATORS
Robert Greisen and Terry Rose
PRINTER
Kenyon Press

The rising popularity of sports-oriented bars and restaurants enticed Kenyon Press to develop a generic line of various tabletop menus and promotional products. Their purpose was to develop something that could be utilized in a variety of situations. They were looking for a menu that would fit as well in a bar where sports were the primary focus, as it would in a hotel lounge with a wide screen TV.

The Sports Mania collection was developed for bars and restaurants desiring to promote more than one athletic event at any given time.

The Sports Locker table tent and popcorn box depict a variety of athletic activities. This allows the operators the opportunity to use only one piece for all sporting events and through each season.

The Sports Grip container is another clever and versatile design which can promote carry-out trade or be used to serve complimentary snacks.

The unique die-cut Clipboard menu holder and screened coordinated sheets allow the management to print the 8½ x 11 inserts in-house.

In developing Top Draft Picks the emphasis was on economy, creativity, flexibility and fun.

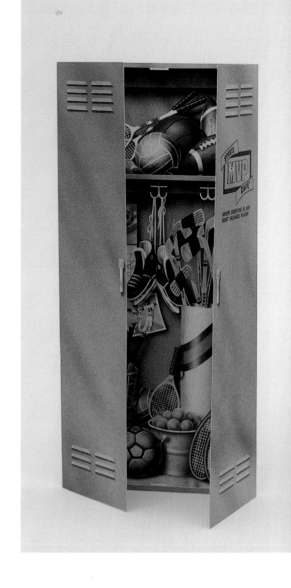

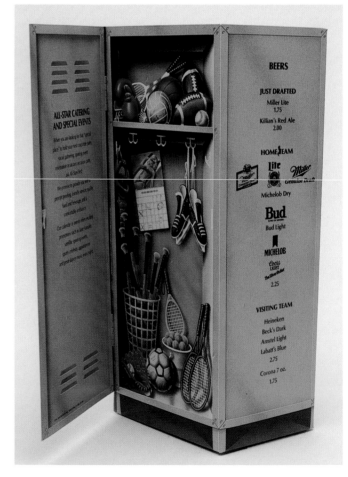

The Breakers Fairways Cafe

RESTAURANT/OPERATOR
The Breakers Fairways Cafe
Palm Beach, FL
YEAR OPENED
1960, renovated 1990
DESIGN FIRM
European Graphics
DESIGNER
Daniel Martin
PRINTER
European Graphics

The Breakers Fairways Cafe dates back to the 1960s, yet the restaurant and resort have been continually updated and repositioned to appeal to a more active clientele. It received a major facelift and renovation in 1990 which included a complete overhaul of the restaurant. The furnishings, window treatments and floor coverings were updated and the restaurant completely repainted. The hotel staff encourages guests to drop in for a bite to eat before or after a round of golf.

The Fairways is the resort's casual cafe and this menu is a graphic representation of the restaurant's look and feel. This menu won Third Place for the "Best Design" in the NRA's 1991 Great Menu Contest.

Cocktail Menu/One Ten Powell

RESTAURANT/OPERATOR
One Ten Powell
Hotel Group of America
San Francisco, CA
YEAR OPENED
1987
DESIGN FIRM
Warren Welter Design
DESIGNER
Warren Welter
ILLUSTRATOR
Callie Peet
PRINTER
Pacific Union College Press

The designer used sculptural pieces from a kit sold at the Museum of Modern Art to create an attractive interactive tabletop menu that doubles as a centerpiece. They are left out for the patrons to play around with so they can build their own unique centerpieces.

Pool Grill

RESTAURANT/OPERATOR
Pool Grill/Grand Hotel
Mackinac Island, MI
YEAR OPENED
1951
DESIGN FIRM
Reeser Advertising Associates
DESIGNER
Nancy C. Reeser
ART DIRECTOR
Nancy C. Reeser
ILLUSTRATOR
Gary Rager
PRINTER
Fidelity Printing

Playing with a beach ball is a casual pool side activity. In an effort to get the attention of guests and increase lunch orders in the pool area, these menus, featuring light fare, were developed. The choice of color is consistent with the restaurant's overall image and works well with the other pieces.

Hang Ten Pool

RESTAURANT/OPERATOR
Hang Ten Pool/Hyatt Regency
Waikoloa, HI
YEAR OPENED
1991
DESIGN FIRM
Kenyon Press
ART DIRECTOR
Pamela Mower-Conner
ILLUSTRATOR
Pamela Mower-Conner
PRINTER
Kenyon Press

A replica of the shirts worn by Hang Ten's wait staff, this custom menu design reflects the bright colors and lush tropical beauty of Hawaii. Sealed-edge laminations for this pool side menu allow for *al fresco* dining amidst the ocean breezes without fear from the salt spray.

CHAPTER
9
Architectural

Cafe La Boheme

RESTAURANT/OPERATOR
Cafe La Boheme
Global Investment Concept
Los Angeles, CA
YEAR OPENED
1991
DESIGN FIRM
Vrontikis Design Office
DESIGNER
Kim Sage
ART DIRECTOR
Petrula Vrontikis
PRINTER
Login Printing
PAPER
matte laminate

The look of Cafe La Boheme is an
eclectic mix of Japanese, Italian and
French styling. The combination of
East meets West is highlighted by an
opulent use of color and texture. The
interior design incorporates sculpture,
mosaics, draperies, lighting, and
furnishings. Also included in the design
package are menus, matches, and
business cards.

Zuni Grill

RESTAURANT/OPERATOR
Zuni Grill/Paesano's Restaurante
San Antonio, TX
YEAR OPENED
1991
DESIGN FIRM
Meridian 28 Design
DESIGNER
Maria Eugenia Garcia
ILLUSTRATOR
Micheal Karshis
PHOTOGRAPHERS
Creston Funk
Al Rendon
PRINTER
Clear Visions/Data Pro

With the design objectives for Zuni Grill two problems needed to be addressed, aesthetics, and the over-whelming client concerns. The needs of the client were first and foremost. The objective was to integrate materials regardless of the specific function of each object. The combined elements all fit together through the use of a common language or design dialog. Once these elements were identified it became a system. For example, the signage is made up of boxes and spheres, the plates are square, the bowls are round, and the wall graphics repeat these uniform patterns. The perforated metal is used in the lighting fixtures, the menu covers and even in the signage. The logotype is made up of jagged letters with an elliptical use of negative space. All the elements relate to each other in a unique and unusual design concept.

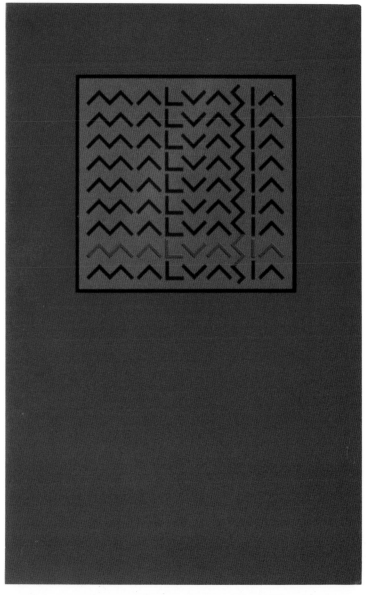

Malvasia

RESTAURANT/OPERATOR
Malvasia
New York, NY
YEAR OPENED
1989
DESIGN FIRM
Monica Banks and Co.
DESIGNER
Monica Banks
ILLUSTRATOR
Monica Banks
COPYWRITER
Gennaro Picone
PRINTER
Darbert Printers

Designed by Adam Tihany, the interior of Malvasia has the look and feel of a stuccoed villa in Sicily. The black wrought iron is patterned with right angles that are a striking contrast against the restaurant's ivory, blue and terra cotta background. The goal was to create a menu with a Mediterranean feeling, one that would reflect the restaurant's look. The logo plays off the use of right angles and the soothing color scheme. The lettering has the look and feel of an ancient Roman stone carving. A bold banner flag prominently hangs atop the building as a unique solution to the problem of exterior signage.

Golden Choice Buffet

RESTAURANT/OPERATOR
Golden Corral
Raleigh, NC
DESIGN FIRM
Dennard Creative, Inc.
DESIGNERS
Bob Dennard, James Lacey,
Chris Wood, June Michel and
Marie St. Hilaire
ILLUSTRATORS
Bob Dennard and James Lacey

Golden Corral is a national chain of steak houses which hired Dennard Creative to update and modernize the image of their graphics. The design firm began by creating a new, more readable logo as well as a pole sign. They then worked to design a new building, one in which older units could be retrofitted for a cohesive look. Door decals were used as a prominent feature at restaurant entryways. The buffet bar features a series of turn-of-the-century signs that help to establish a sense of heritage for the restaurant. There are also more utilitarian signs designed to meet municipal regulations. The Golden Corral has a comfortable look that reaches back to the past, without being lost in it.

NEW! THE GOLDEN CHOICE BUFFET™
(It's a whole new meal everyday!)

EVERY TUESDAY!
SHRIMPFEST™
EXTRAVAGANZA

INTRODUCING
golden corral
TO GO
MENU

Now you can enjoy our tasty Golden Choice Buffet™ at home on-the-go. Everything available – our fresh hot soups, the huge baked potatoes and our wonderful desserts. And don't fresh-baked rolls, cookies from bakery! many of our regu- too! Including Golden our USDA Golden Corral – thy, delicious, ble. And now – to go!

golden corral

Blackhawk Grille

RESTAURANT/OPERATOR
Blackhawk Grille
California Restaurant Group
Danville, CA
YEAR OPENED
1990
DESIGN FIRM
Tharp Did It!
DESIGNER
Jana Heer, Jean Mogannam and Kim Tomlinson
ART DIRECTOR
Rick Tharp
PRINTER
Zenith Printing

The Blackhawk Grille is located near a classic car museum. A different auto is featured in the bar area each month. Subtle references to automotive design and technology were combined with an Art Deco logotype to give the restaurant the feel of a bygone era. A by-the-glass wine board was fabricated from a sheet of galvanized aluminum and silkscreened with the available names. The frame was built into the wall and covered with the same handmade paper that was used. All menus and graphics utilize a background pattern created from a photograph of the surface of an adobe wall.

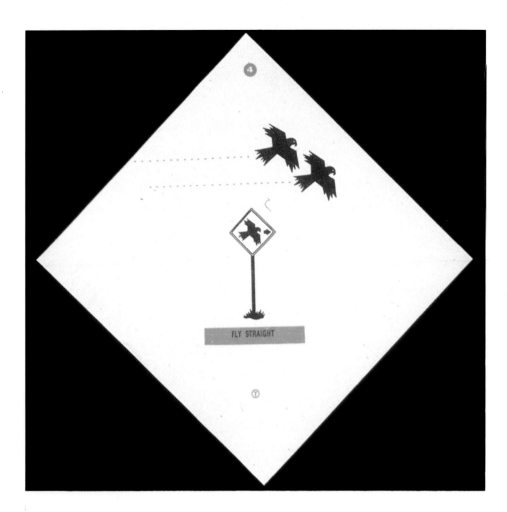

WINTER

DINNER

MENU

SPRING

DINNER

MENU

SUMMER

DINNER

MENU

FALL

DINNER

MENU

Cypress Club

RESTAURANT/OPERATOR
Cypress Club
New Vision Restaurant
Partners
San Francisco, CA
YEAR OPENED
1990
DESIGN FIRM
Diane Dias Design
DESIGNER
Diane Dias
PHOTOGRAPHER
Mitchell Shenker
ILLUSTRATORS
Diane Dias & Jordan Mozer
PRINTER
Forman Leibrock

The Cypress Club is an architectural fantasy set with sweeping expanses of rounded copper partitions and doorways, voluptuous glass fixtures, and sensual shapes. It has a cartoon-like quality, a 1940s industrial look mixed with touches of Art Nouveau and unabashed creativity. Although an overwhelming visual extravaganza, it somehow manages to make it all work together.

The key was to carefully balance the menu design with the restaurant's interior. The introduction of a whimsical "mark," suggested by the chef and inspired by architect Jordan Mozer's stained glass window would become the connecting element. The undulating architecture was transformed into a wavy border reminiscent of the kind of Art Nouveau embellishments done at the turn-of-the-century. Random varnish and spot UV patterns were used to create a subtle texture.

The wine list book is made from an attractive handmade paper imported from France. The designer experimented with various metal fasteners, wire, and even buttons to create an elegant, yet industrial look for the binding.

150

151

Bix

RESTAURANT/OPERATOR
Bix/Alley Associates
San Francisco, CA
YEAR OPENED
1988
DESIGNER
Jim Moon (menu design)
ILLUSTRATOR
Rod Dyer (logo and illustrations)

Bix is a jazzy back alley supper club in San Francisco's financial district. It occupies a historic Gold Rush era building. However, many of the design cues are Art Deco in style, including the menu graphics. But the architect, Michael Guthrie, points out that different styles were mixed to create something with more impact. Behind the bar, a contemporary mural by architect Mindy Lehrman, depicts a jazz band and crowded dance floor, It represents an idealized image of a night out at Bix. The original logo design was created by Rod Dyer of Los Angeles.

CIII Restaurant

RESTAURANT/OPERATOR
CIII Restaurant
Washington Square Hotel
New York, NY
YEAR OPENED
1991
DESIGN FIRM
PM Design and Marketing
Communications
DESIGNER
Philip Marzo

There were two primary considerations in developing a menu for CIII, a Greenwich Village restaurant, located in the Washington Square Hotel. First, the menu needed to reflect the sophisticated mix of color, texture and materials that the architect and owners had chosen. This was accomplished through the creative use of a silkscreen on parchment paper. Fabric covered eyehooks were used to connect the menu sleeves. Second, the menu needed to be flexible. As CIII evolves, its owners want to be able to incorporate menu changes that reflect client and marketplace findings. Several menu templates were designed to simplify the effects of changing food and wine selections each day. Durable heavy gauge plastic sleeves protect the menu and allow for the easy insertion of revised menus.

CIII

DINNER SPECIALS

WINES BY THE GLASS
Wine Special 1...$4.00
Wine Special 2...$4.50

SOUPS
Chunky Chicken Barley with Wild Mushrooms
    and Thyme..$3.75

APPETIZERS
Endive Arugula and Warm Beets with Toasted
    Walnut and Blue Cheese Vinaigrette.............$4.25
Smoked Trout Potato Pancakes with Horseradish
    Apple Sauce...$5.00
Roasted Peppers, Anchovies and Olives with
    Grilled Country Bread................................$4.25

ENTREES
Roast Pepper and Grilled Eggplant Lasagna
    with Herbed Ricotta and Feta Bechamel.........
Pan Roasted Cod with Artichokes and Black O
    Tapenade..
Mixed Seafood Risotto with Lobster B
Roasted Leg of Lamb, Cous-Co
    Eggplant Compote...........

DESSERT
Mom's Cake wi

SI

CIII

MENU

SOUPS
Bean and Roasted Garlic Soup....................$3.25
Lobster Broth with Seafood Dumplings........$4.00

APPETIZERS
Mixed Field Greens with Roasted Leek
    Vinaigrette...$4.75
Layered Vegetable and Sheep Cheese
    Terrine with Lemon Basil Oil......................$4.75
Thai Pepper Glazed Salmon over Bitter
    Greens with Lemon Grass..........................$5.50
Crispy Calamari with Shrimp Chili Sauce.........$5.25

SANDWICHES
Grilled Chicken with Grilled Zucchini, Sweet Onion
    and Olive Mayonnaise on Sourdough Bread..$7.25
Roasted Eggplant and Chickpea Burrito
    with Avocado Cucumber Relish.................$6.50

A
Pumpkin Filled Ravioli with Wild Mushrooms
    and Kale..$9.00
Linguini with Roasted Winter Vegetables and
    Crispy Filet of Flounder...........................$10.25

Chicken, Mashed Potatoes and Roasted Garlic
    y with Fragrant Green of the Day.......$10.50
    ish with Grilled Vegetables with
    Aioli......................................$13.50
    n, and Bean of the Day Plate..........$8.25
    Rib Eye Beef with Sweet Potato
    reens...................................$15.00
    ries....................................$7.95

    h Corn and
    ....$16.00

CIII
Restaurant
at the
Washington Square Hotel

MENU

Cafe Toma

RESTAURANT/OPERATOR
Cafe Toma/Tom Duffy
San Francisco, CA
YEAR OPENED
1991
DESIGN FIRM
Bruce Yelaska Design
DESIGNER
Bruce Yelaska
PRINTER
Vision Printing

Cafe Toma is located in the SoMa District of San Francisco, an area known for its artists and nightclubs. The logo design was inspired by the architect's use of an eclectic mix of industrial materials along with newly designed items. A wide variety of elements served as inspiration including painted surfaces and a wall mural. The enlarged spiral makes for an inviting front cover. It serves to reinforce the logo also used on the cover. The simple angular cuts on the top and bottom of the menu and on stationery were inspired by a wooden wall at the front of the restaurant. The wall is diagonally cut and inlaid in contrasting woods. The menu typography is simple and easy to read. The one-color menus are printed on an off-white recycled stock and capture the restaurant's industrial look, but with contemporary verve. To further enhance this mood, the signage uses a variety of metal surfaces and different colored neon in a powerful, but controlled manner.

CAFÉ
T°MA

APPETIZERS

Italian sausage, roasted peppers and marinara sauce 4.95
Cold calamari salad with vinaigrette 4.95
Roasted whole garlic head, feta cheese, kalamata olives,
  marinated artichoke hearts and peperoncini 4.95
Roasted whole garlic head, mozzarella cheese, salame and peperoncini 5.25

SALADS

House salad—hearts of romaine, currants and roasted walnuts 3.50
Caesar salad 4.50
Cold pasta—capellini with smoked chicken 4.50
Cold pasta—capellini with vegetables . . . .
Tuna salad . . . . APPE
  *crumbled blue cheese add . . . .85¢

FOCACCIA BREAD S

Ham and ch
Italian saus
Chicken bre
Roast loin o
Swordfish st
Salmon . . . .

    sandwiches
    roasted pep

HOUSE SPEC

Half roasted garli
Roast loin of pork
Eggplant parmigiana
Prawns marinara wit.

PASTA

Tortellini—aurora sauc
Tortellini—pesto sauce
Rigatoni—small veal mea
Rigatoni—italian sausage,
Capellini—prima vera . . .
Capellini—pesto . . . .

Visa—Mastercard
Please no cigars/pipes/clove cigarettes
Thanx—

158

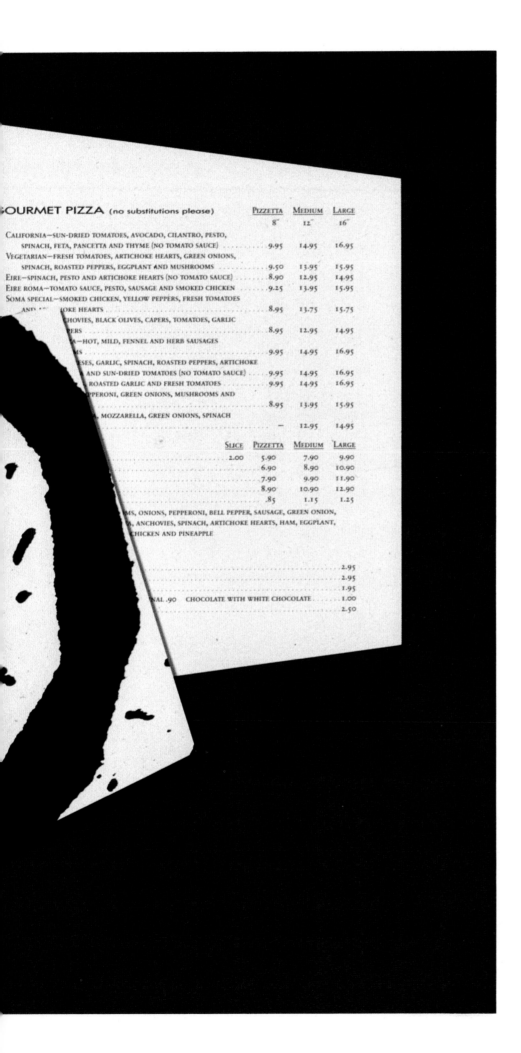

GOURMET PIZZA (no substitutions please)

	PIZZETTA 8"	MEDIUM 12"	LARGE 16"
CALIFORNIA—SUN-DRIED TOMATOES, AVOCADO, CILANTRO, PESTO, SPINACH, FETA, PANCETTA AND THYME (NO TOMATO SAUCE)	9.95	14.95	16.95
VEGETARIAN—FRESH TOMATOES, ARTICHOKE HEARTS, GREEN ONIONS, SPINACH, ROASTED PEPPERS, EGGPLANT AND MUSHROOMS	9.50	13.95	15.95
EIRE—SPINACH, PESTO AND ARTICHOKE HEARTS (NO TOMATO SAUCE)	8.90	12.95	14.95
EIRE ROMA—TOMATO SAUCE, PESTO, SAUSAGE AND SMOKED CHICKEN	9.25	13.95	15.95
SOMA SPECIAL—SMOKED CHICKEN, YELLOW PEPPERS, FRESH TOMATOES AND ◌◌◌◌ OKE HEARTS	8.95	13.75	15.75
◌◌◌ CHOVIES, BLACK OLIVES, CAPERS, TOMATOES, GARLIC ◌◌ERS	8.95	12.95	14.95
◌◌A—HOT, MILD, FENNEL AND HERB SAUSAGES ◌◌S	9.95	14.95	16.95
◌◌ESES, GARLIC, SPINACH, ROASTED PEPPERS, ARTICHOKE ◌◌ AND SUN-DRIED TOMATOES (NO TOMATO SAUCE)	9.95	14.95	16.95
◌◌ ROASTED GARLIC AND FRESH TOMATOES	9.95	14.95	16.95
◌◌PPERONI, GREEN ONIONS, MUSHROOMS AND ◌◌	8.95	13.95	15.95
◌◌, MOZZARELLA, GREEN ONIONS, SPINACH ◌◌	—	12.95	14.95

	SLICE	PIZZETTA	MEDIUM	LARGE
◌◌	2.00	5.90	7.90	9.90
◌◌		6.90	8.90	10.90
◌◌		7.90	9.90	11.90
◌◌		8.90	10.90	12.90
◌◌	.85	1.15	1.25

◌◌MS, ONIONS, PEPPERONI, BELL PEPPER, SAUSAGE, GREEN ONION,
◌◌A, ANCHOVIES, SPINACH, ARTICHOKE HEARTS, HAM, EGGPLANT,
◌◌ CHICKEN AND PINEAPPLE

◌◌ 2.95
◌◌ 2.95
◌◌ 1.95
◌◌NAL .90   CHOCOLATE WITH WHITE CHOCOLATE 1.00
◌◌ 2.50

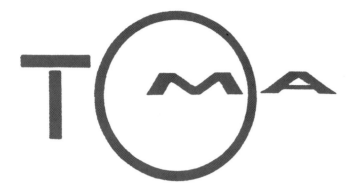

CAFÉ TOMA

CAFÉ TOMA

CAFÉ TOMA

CAFÉ TOMA

CAFÉ TOMA

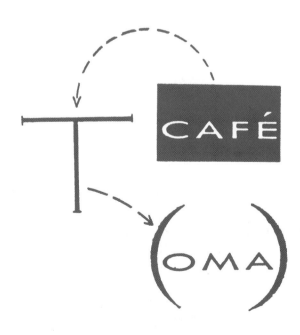

CAFÉ TOMA
371 11TH STREET
SAN FRANCISCO, CALIFO
RNIA 94103
PHONE 252.5320
FAX 252.5322

CALIFORNIA 9410

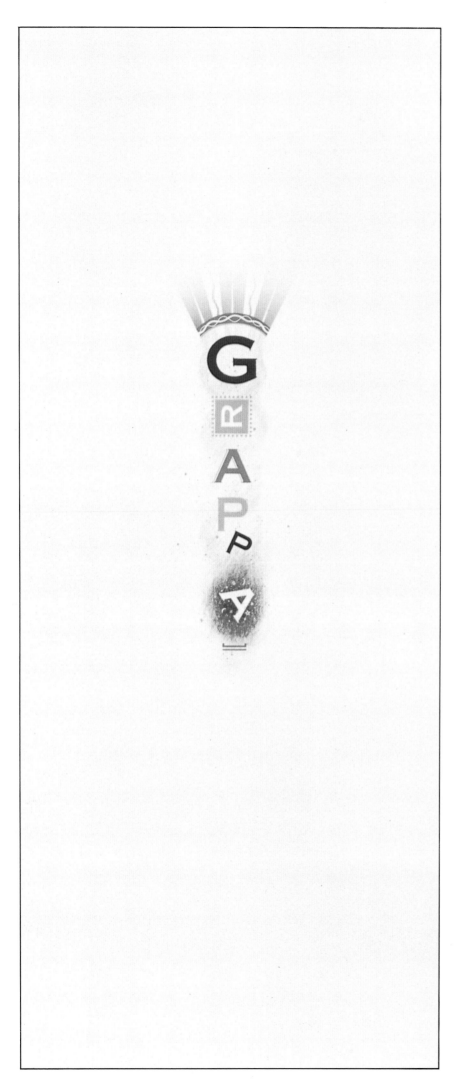

Grappa

RESTAURANT/OPERATOR
Grappa
St. Louis, MO
YEAR OPENED
1990
DESIGN FIRM
Heller Rosenfeld Design
DESIGNER
Julie Rosenfeld
ILLUSTRATOR
Julie Rosenfeld
PRINTER
Dale Printing Co.

The clean, crisp window sign at
Grappa establishes a refined mood for
the restaurant even from the street.
Located in the historic Pierce Arrow
building in St. Louis' urbane Central
West End, the emphasis here is on the
food. Lou Reed, the chef and one of
the partners involved in the restaurant
has placed the importance on quality
and freshness. He uses only organically
grown meats and produce in simply
prepared meals that use unusual
combinations. The result is a clean but
elegant departure from the traditional.

It was designer Julie Rosenfeld's
intention to create a logo that would
complement Grappa's philosophy. She
customized it by working with a
beautiful old type, Copperplate, and
then modifying each character to
appear differently from the rest. Some
letters are smaller than others, some
are turned one way or another, one is
even lying on its side. The letters are
all held together in a floating cloud
done in varying shades of blue. It is
capped with a crown and ray motif
reminiscent of the Statue of Liberty
that enlivens the design. On the other
hand, the interior of the menu is crisp
and conservative, a simple design that
successfully keeps the emphasis on
the food.

Route 66 Roadhouse and Cantina

RESTAURANT/OPERATOR
Route 66 Roadhouse and Cantina
Boca Raton, FL
DESIGN FIRM
David Savage/Art & Design
DESIGNER
David Savage
ILLUSTRATOR
David Savage
PHOTOGRAPHER
David Savage
PRINTER
Boca Raton Printing Company

The Route 66 motto, "if you're not having fun...don't blame us," sums up the restaurant's generally playful philosophy. In fact, opportunities to make plays on the theme are rarely missed. Cows are a major interior design element, old road signs are present everywhere. Historic photographs of oddities found along Route 66 and old neon signs adorn the walls. Interior architectural elements are clad in corrugated metal or white-washed clapboard siding. Booth seating is rolled and pleated Naugahyde. The wait staff wears mechanic's overalls embroidered with imaginery names, with "Gomer" being a popular choice.

Never passing up an opportunity to enhance the Route 66 theme, the menu folds like a road map. It was created to be a throw-away because the designer realized nobody would get it folded back the right way. Menu selections are handwritten over faded roadside images thus reinforcing the restaurant's casual roadhouse feel. On the reverse side is a souvenir map of old Route 66 with a "you are here," insert included so nobody gets confused. November 11, 1992 will mark the 66th anniversary of this restaurant.

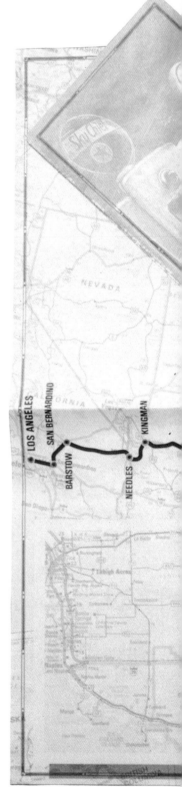

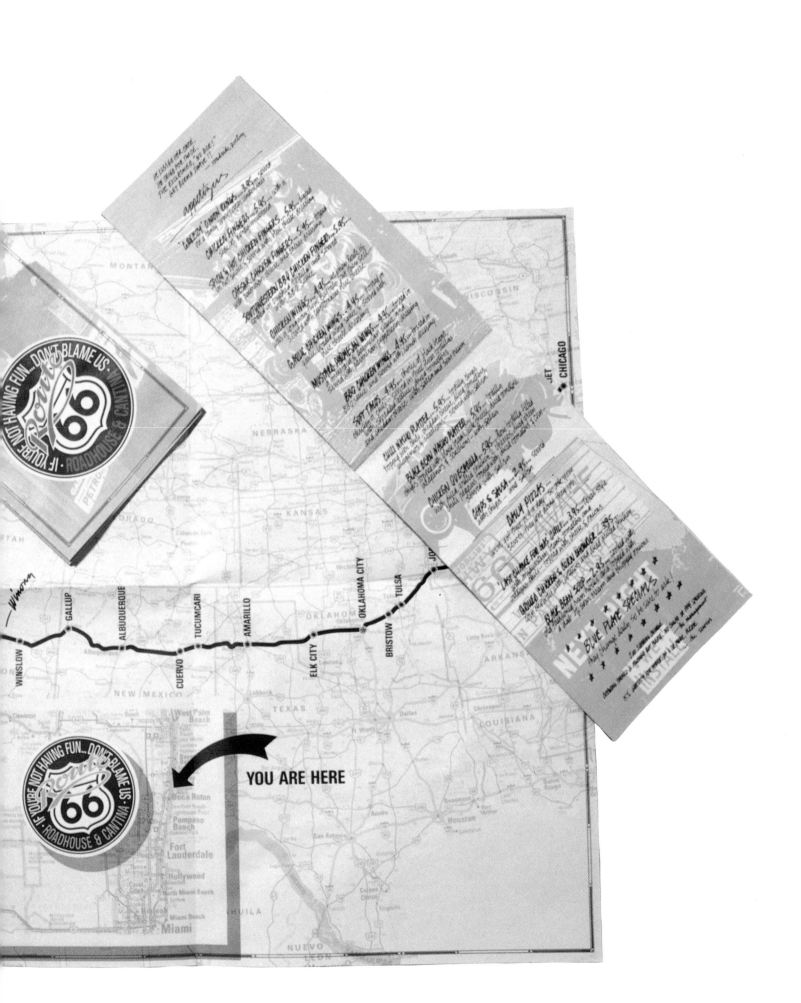

YOU ARE HERE

CHAPTER 10

Hotels/ Catering

Omni Melrose

RESTAURANT/OPERATOR
Omni Melrose/Omni International Dallas, TX
YEAR OPENED
1927
DESIGN FIRM
Baker & Grooms
DESIGNERS
Mikie Baker and Lindy Grooms
ILLUSTRATOR
Fred Henley
PRINTER
Allcraft Printing

Opened 65 years ago, the Omni Melrose is a historic landmark in Dallas. Since windows are a prominent feature, the designer, Mikie Baker wanted to use views taken from various rooms and illustrated by artist Fred Henley. It was a way of promoting the hotel to both guests and local customers alike. The dining room called for menus that could be easily updated, but that would be compatible with its upscale image. A postcard was designed as part of the hotel's graphics system to be used as a promotional tool.

Shaklee San Francisco
Convention Banquet

RESTAURANT/OPERATOR
Shaklee San Francisco
Convention Banquet
San Francisco, CA
DESIGN FIRM
Jim Hurd Design
DESIGNER
Jim Jasdine
ART DIRECTOR
Jim Hurd
ILLUSTRATOR
Rick Van Genderen
PRINTER
South Park Press

This menu was used as a place setting at the final banquet for the Shaklee Company's convention held in San Francisco. This piece, a collaboration between designer Jim Hurd and illustrator Rick Van Genderen, established a look for the evening. The illustration, a view of the city's skyline was used on all of the nine pieces in the campaign. Each one was handled in a slightly different way. For the

menu illustration, a nighttime scene was used. Mr. Hurd was inspired during a recent trip to Paris by the Louvre Museum Pyramid designed by I.M. Pei. He devised a series of simple folds so the menu would work as a stand-up piece. Two sides of it were die-cut so the front edges would lay flat. In the process this single-sided printed piece was transformed into an unusual three-dimensional menu.

"Shiftin' Gears"
Radisson Plaza Hotel

RESTAURANT/OPERATOR
Radisson Plaza Hotel at
Town Center
Radisson Hotel Corporation
Southfield, MI
YEAR OPENED
1987
DESIGN FIRM
Hetland Ltd.
DESIGNER
Douglas Fliss
ART DIRECTOR
Douglas Fliss
PHOTOGRAPHER
Russ Hanson
AIRBRUSHING
Roger Peterson
PRINTER
Kaye's Printing

This high concept piece, done for the Radisson Plaza Hotel at Town Center in Southfield, Michigan, was planned to create a visually exciting context for group sales meeting breaks. Done with a nostalgic automobile theme, it divides the selections from the lower cost alternatives to the top-of-the-line menu choices. Each is given a different title, and the food items are highlighted. There is a small amount of explanatory text, playful in nature and designed to pay tribute to the brochure's "car crazy" theme. The hotel is positioned as the market's top-flight property, with heavy stress on originality and service.

Salle a Manager Grand Hotel

RESTAURANT/OPERATOR
Salle a Manager/Grand Hotel
Mackinac Island, MI
YEAR OPENED
1887
DESIGN FIRM
Reeser Advertising Associates
DESIGNER
Nancy C. Reeser
ART DIRECTOR
Nancy C. Reeser
ILLUSTRATOR
Jeff Landis
PRINTER
Graphics 3

This menu celebrates the 100th anniversary of The Grand Hotel on Mackinac Island in Michigan. Built in 1887, it is America's oldest summer resort. The client wanted something that would capture the spirit of summer, be functional, and that could act as a memento. Because of the resort's seasonality, the designer wanted to emphasize the Fourth of July, a summer holiday traditionally celebrated with parades. The flag and confetti motif is the essence of the summer holiday season. The interior features a pop-up of the historic hotel known for its portico with its sweeping views. Since no automobiles are allowed on the island, transportation is limited to old-fashioned horse drawn hackney coaches like the one shown. A furling flag makes up the background.

Banquet Menu for Hyatt Regency Maui

RESTAURANT/OPERATOR
Hyatt Regency Maui
Lahaina, Maui, HI
DESIGN FIRM
Associates
DESIGNER
Chutintorn Satthum
ART DIRECTOR
Bobbie Warehan
ILLUSTRATOR
Bobbie Warehan
PRINTER
Associates

The resort's tropical atmosphere led to the design of this multi-layered, multi-textured design for the Hyatt Regency Maui. The cover's sea shell design is continued in the interior of the menu as well with a variety of die-cut shells creating a paradigm for the hotel's banquet and dining services.

Room Service Menu, Holiday Inn Mart Plaza

RESTAURANT/OPERATOR
Holiday Inn Mart Plaza
Chicago, IL
DESIGN FIRM
Associates
DESIGNER
Jill Varvil
ILLUSTRATOR
Jill Varvil
PRINTER
Associates

This stylish menu for the Holiday Inn Mart Plaza, located adjacent to Chicago's famous Apparel Center and near the Merchandise Mart, reflects the small hotel's sophisticated clientele. A pleasant departure from the usual, this highly stylized graphic owes a debt of gratitude to Art Deco, but has an updated look that is pure '90s.

It won a First Place in the 1991 NRA award in the "Banquet/Catering" category.

Room Service Menu for Hotel Vintage Plaza

RESTAURANT/OPERATOR
Hotel Vintage Plaza
Kimco Hotel Management
San Francisco, CA
YEAR OPENED
1990
DESIGN FIRM
Warren Welter Design
DESIGNER
Warren Welter
ILLUSTRATOR
Christine Cuccia
PRINTER
Roger Patterson

In order to use the four-color logo on all collateral pieces without incurring the expense of four-color printing, a large quantity of stickers were printed. The Hotel Vintage Plaza had the housekeeping staff apply stickers to the menus. The grape leaf die-cut allows the piece to be hung on the door knob.

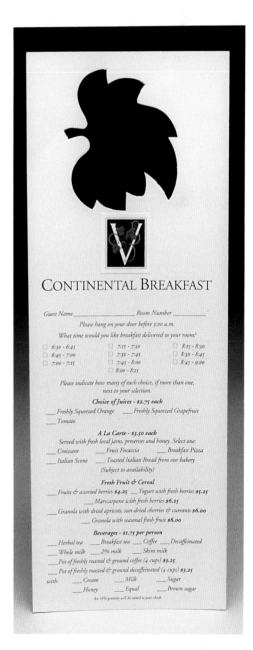

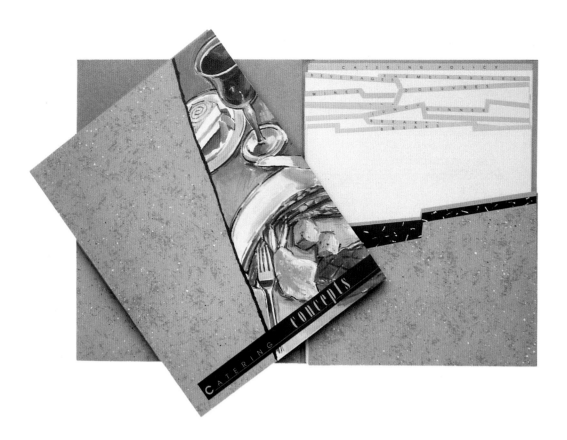

Banquet Menu and Inserts for Ramada Renaissance

RESTAURANT/OPERATOR
Ramada Renaissance North America
Phoenix, AZ
YEAR OPENED
1991
DESIGN FIRM
Kenyon Press
DESIGNER
Pamela Mower-Conner
ILLUSTRATOR
Pamela Mower-Conner
PRINTER
Kenyon Press

Due to cost considerations, Ramada International requested an alternative to mailing the complete menu package to every client requesting catering information. The hotel was instrumental in the design direction this project took. They wanted to create a menu consisting of a folder and individually graded inserts with four-color art work on each piece. This allowed the hotel's catering department to project a positive image whether sending a full kit or a single page. Careful attention was given to the subject matter of each illustration to insure that all categories would be accurately represented. The illustrations were chosen to appeal to a wide variety of tastes; it also needed to be generic enough that other hotels in the chain could make use of this attractive system.

New Otani Hotel

RESTAURANT/OPERATOR
New Otani Hotel
New Otani America
Los Angeles, CA
YEAR OPENED
1977
DESIGN FIRM
COY, Los Angeles
DESIGNER
Laurie Handler
ART DIRECTOR
John Coy
PRINTER
Thousand Oaks Printing

This folder system, designed for the New Otani Hotel in Los Angeles, is used for handling the in-room menu, the hotel directory, a letterhead folder with stationery and other inserts. The package needed to coordinate with the existing interior color scheme and make a simple, elegant statement. Bound with a dusty rose silk cord, it is printed in both English and Japanese for a room service system with a distinctly oriental flavor.

Banquet Folder and Inserts,
Hyatt at Fisherman's Wharf

RESTAURANT/OPERATOR
Hyatt at Fisherman's Wharf
San Francisco, CA
DESIGN FIRM
Kenyon Press
DESIGNER
Ara Keoshkerian
ILLUSTRATOR
Michelle Manning
PRINTER
Kenyon Press

Felix Solomon, food and beverage director of the Hyatt Fisherman's Wharf, requested a banquet folder that would be not only an attractive sales tool but would also allow him to make changes in the menu.

A pastel rendering of the Palace of the Fine Arts was chosen to grace the front cover because of its prominence as a local landmark. The cover's rich hues and dreamlike quality mirror the hotel's colors and relaxing atmosphere. "We duplicated the pastel rendering," Mr. Solomon said. "And we screened the image onto the inserts in order to continue the tranquil feeling and unite the whole piece." The background is an actual scan of a new paper stock, Curtis Brightwater Marble Crema Cover, the perfect backdrop for an architectural subject. Menu inserts provided the flexibility Mr. Solomon requested.

CHAPTER 11

Casual Dining

Chancery Pub and Restaurant

RESTAURANT/OPERATOR
Chancery Pub and Restaurant/
De Rosa Corporation
Wauwatosa, WI
DESIGN FIRM
Miller Meester Advertising and
Z Studio Design & Illustration
DESIGNER
Matt Zumbo
ART DIRECTOR
Doug Engel
ILLUSTRATOR
Matt Zumbo
PRINTER
Sells Printing

Located in Wauwatosa, Wisconsin, the Chancery Pub uses this menu to poke fun at the Dairy State's number one position in cheese production. The objective was to instantly translate the restaurant's identity the minute a guest laid eyes on the menu. A colloquial style self-depracating humor was the order of the day.

The front cover features two outrageous cartoon characters with exaggerated heads. One, with a large cheese wedge for a head is playing the piano. The other, bikini-clad with a tomato for a head is perched atop the

piano. The caption reads "It's Cheesehead Mambo Time," and refers to a regional nickname for Wisconsin residents. Chancery's menu shows a nice blending of copy and distraction, with easy-to-read, well-marked selections. It's a fun menu to look at, as well as read, and sets the tone for an enjoyable meal.

Chancery Pub was a 1991 NRA winner in three categories. They won a Second Place for restaurants with an "Average Check Under $8." They also won Second Place in the "Greatest Merchandising Power" category and a Second Place in "Best Design."

Hollywood Canteen

RESTAURANT/OPERATOR
Hollywood Canteen
Los Angeles, CA
YEAR OPENED
1991
DESIGN FIRM
Jim Heimann Design
DESIGNER
Jim Heimann
PRINTER
Independent Projects Press

The Hollywood Canteen commissioned Jim Heimann to do the work because they were trying to recreate a grill circa 1939. The designer has demonstrated his knowledge by writing several books about old Hollywood and also one on matchbook covers. The interior and exterior of the restaurant reflect that period even to the point of duplicating the booths of the old Brown Derby restaurant. The menu cover was intended to appear as though it was designed in the late '30s; Mr. Heimann used his extensive collection of old menus in the research. To duplicate the "old look" as closely as possible, the covers were printed by letterpress, a process that relies on hand manipulation more than offset. The individual matchsticks were printed as matches would have been in that era, thus making them a collector's item.

Bruce Licher of Independent Projects Press, known for using the letterpress to achieve a vintage look and for his fine craftsmanship, was responsible for the printing. The inconsistencies of letterpress and large ink coverage were exploited and flaws in the process were emphasized to accurately reflect the problems of the period. The matches followed this same process. Lion Match Company of Chicago did the printing and fabrication. The first run was rejected because the paper stock was too slick. The designer wound up providing a special paper, one that absorbed the ink and softened the look. The mechanical art contained deliberate flaws intended to capture the true look and feel of a 1939 print job.

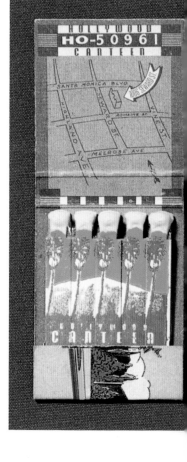

Zachary's Dinner Menu

RESTAURANT/OPERATOR
Zachary's/Colonnade Hotel
Boston, MA
YEAR OPENED
1971
PRINTER
Carol Printing

At Zachary's, the fine dining establishment at the Colonnade Hotel, Chef Ripperger has created a unique theme for the menu of this 21-year-old restaurant. The concept is rooted in ancient notions of the way the world was viewed. The menu layout is arranged into four elements: FIRE, AIR, EARTH, WATER. By arranging the menu layout into these four elemental categories, dishes that are flame broiled or smoked fall under the FIRE category. Lighter dishes and those that make use of winged creatures fall under the heading of AIR. The EARTH Category makes use of those that are harvested from the ground and animals that roam upon it. Foods found in or upon WATER are listed under that category. There is also a "tasting menu" that combines items from all four categories.

179

B.J.'s, A Place for Ribs

RESTAURANT/OPERATOR
B.J.'s, A Place for Ribs
Selingsgrove, PA
DESIGN FIRM
Newton Advertising, Inc.
DESIGNER
Steve Newton
ART DIRECTOR
Linda Newton
ILLUSTRATORS
Cora Lynn Deibler and Patty Argoff
PHOTOGRAPHER
Terry Wild
PRINTER
Reed-Hann Litho

Once a laid back place for ribs, B.J.'s success grew to include two locations in Pennsylvania. Through the process of growth and expansion they found that they had diluted their identity. The new menu for the restaurant was created as a close collaboration between the client and designer Linda Newton. The agency's goal was to get back to basics and create graphics that would be fun and visually exciting. Produced from cut-out colored paper shapes which were then photographed, the menu printing was done on a six-color press. It features B.J.'s now famous pink pig, also used in the restaurant's new signage. A new look for the resturant's wait staff was also created; the new outfits combine khakis with a pin-striped shirt and creative neckties.

The changes have increased business by up to 20 percent at both locations. Bob Kirkpatrick, the owner, credits the graphics and continues to reinforce the new image with a strong use of in-house promotions backed by a matching print campaign. "I was nervous about such a dramatic change," he says, "but it has produced great results. Nothing else could have saved us. Today people perceive us as a fun place with good food and an excellent value."

This menu is a 1991 National Restaurant Association winner having taken "Second Place in the Most Imaginative" category.

Border Grill

RESTAURANT/OPERATOR
The Border Grill
St. Louis, MO
YEAR OPENED
1991
DESIGN FIRM
Heller Rosenfeld Design
DESIGNER
Julie Rosenfeld
ILLUSTRATOR
Julie Rosenfeld
PRINTER
Maritz, Inc.

The Border Grill in Saint Louis wanted to create an explosive logo that could be used to enhance the restaurant's interior. The logo, shaped like an explosion, is a dynamic graphic emblazoned in red with the restaurant's name. It is repeated in the custom-made light fixtures and was even painted on the floor. The menus are nicely accented and were customized by using red trim plastic menu covers.

Chili's

RESTAURANT/OPERATOR
Chili's Grill & Bar
Brinker International
Dallas, TX
YEAR OPENED
1975
DESIGN FIRM
S.B.G. Partners
DESIGNER
Veronica Denny
ILLUSTRATOR
Dave Danz
PRINTER
RM Graphics

Family-oriented fun is graphically represented by the wood-cut style treatment of this menu for the Chili's Bar and Grill chain. The client wanted a menu that would present a clean design, while capturing the restaurant's Southwestern spirit. Printed on a synthetic material to preserve the menu's life for these busy restaurants, the intent was to simplify and clarify selections.

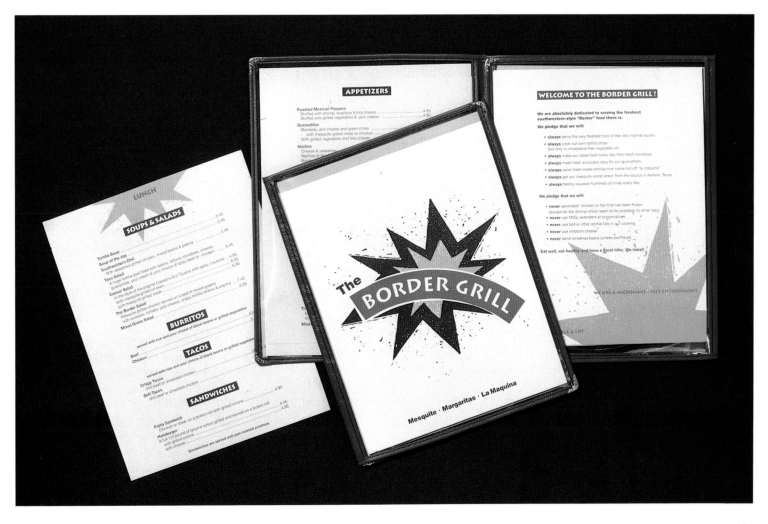

Lime Rickey's Food & Bar Menus

RESTAURANT/OPERATOR
Lime Rickey's Restaurant
Prime Restaurant Group
Mississauga, Ontario, Canada
YEAR OPENED
1985
DESIGN FIRM
Marbury Advertising
Communications
ART DIRECTOR
Heather Gentleman
ILLUSTRATOR
Bill Boyko
PRINTER
Spirit Graphics

The dynamic design of this menu echoes the key architectural elements of the restaurant. The designer used posterized images of the restaurant's interior to create a high contrast graphic effect that adds a striking design element to the layout. All this works well to convey the diner of the '90s image of Lime Rickey's.

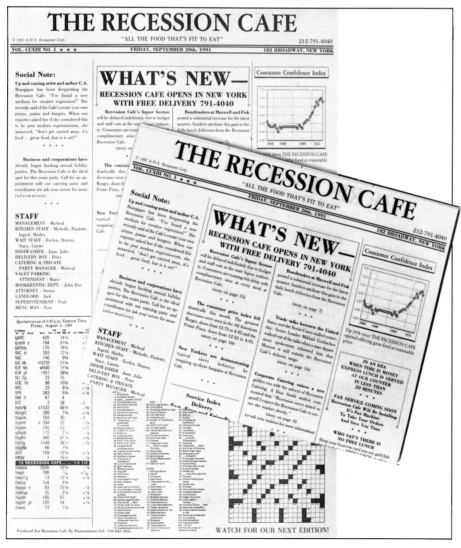

The Recession Cafe

RESTAURANT/OPERATOR
The Recession Cafe
New York, NY
DESIGN FIRM
Presentations Ltd.
DESIGNER
Thomas Vlahakis
PRINTER
F&T Graphics

The Recession Cafe, located in New York's Wall Street area, has a menu that was cleverly designed to resemble the *Wall Street Journal*. This newspaper-style format provides a quick presentation of the food selection and includes cleverly written text. Actually printed on newsprint, it is then laminated to withstand wear and tear. Thomas Vlahakis, the menu's designer, mentioned that this was one of his only samples ever "stolen" at the restaurant show.

Willie C's Cafe & Bar

RESTAURANT/OPERATOR
Willie C's Cafe & Bar
Wichita, KS
DESIGN FIRM
Blick Benest & Co.
DESIGNER
Gary Benest
ILLUSTRATOR
Gary Benest
PRINTER
Quality Printing

At Willie C's in Wichita, the exterior resembles a roadside cafe designed with numerous gables to appear as though several additions have been added to the original structure. They wanted to develop a concept that would portray the friendly, casual atmosphere of a West-Texas cafe. So it is no surprise that the luncheon counter became the restaurant's central focus. The interiors are well lit and feature memorabilia from the '40s and '50s as well as a number of neon signs. The background music is comprised of classic oldies. The wait staff wears denim shorts, casual pullovers and aprons. Hostesses wear denim shorts and bowling shirts.

The adjoining stores are decorated with post-war era artifacts that lend a nostalgic feeling and complement the restaurant's fun atmosphere.

In order to minimize long-term production costs, menu shells that allow for product and price changes were used. All graphics, including advertising materials, maintain a flip sense of humor to further promote the overall experience.

Willie C's was a 1991 NRA First Place winner in the "Average Check Under $8" category.

Cafe Lulu

RESTAURANT/OPERATOR
Cafe Lulu
Kansas City, MO
YEAR OPENED
1989
DESIGN FIRM
Muller & Company
DESIGNER
Patrice Eilts
ART DIRECTORS
John Muller and Patrice Eilts
ILLUSTRATORS
Patrice Eilts and Sarah Rolloff
PRINTER
Ashcraft Printing

Stepping into Cafe Lulu in Kansas City, you realize it is unlike any restaurant you have ever been in before. The atmosphere is intimate, friendly, and familiar. Lu Jane Temple, the proprietress and head chef, refers to the cuisine as, "World Food," influenced by several different international traditions.

The logo and graphics reflect the intriguing interior design. A fold art rendition of Lu Jane standing in front of her restaurant was used on the menu cover. It also appears on a poster and on an oversized postcard. All graphic materials filled one press sheet and are printed in four-color. Included were the menu, the poster, two different-sized postcards, note cards, table tents and even coasters. The menu itself received flood UV coating, while the remaining pieces received spot-coating, assuming the black plate as its own. The menu is a narrow pocket folder designed to accommodate the quarterly cuisine alterations, as well as to make constant changes in the wine list. The restaurant also uses the menu's pockets to hold flyers advertising frequent entertainment events, such as live comedy, amateur jazz night, and poetry readings.

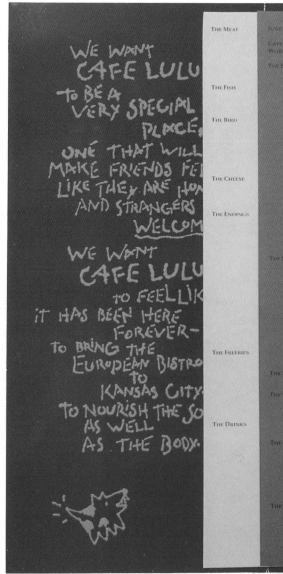

184

Cafe Del Rey

RESTAURANT/OPERATOR
Cafe Del Rey
California Restaurant Group
Marina Del Rey, CA
YEAR OPENED
1991
DESIGN FIRM
Tharp Did It!
DESIGNERS
Eric Enstrom, Barbara Hofling,
Jean Mogannam and Rick Tharp
ART DIRECTOR
Rick Tharp
ILLUSTRATORS
Rick Tharp and Jean Mogannam
PRINTER
Zenith Printing

This logotype was inspired by the restaurant's proximity to the boat basin in the Marina Del Rey section of Los Angeles. The individual letter-forms are reminiscent of the mainsails and spinnakers seen in the harbor. But, they are also derivative of the Italian barrel-back chairs selected by the interior designers. The perforated metal screening used in the vaulted ceiling served as inspiration for the menu's backdrop.

Lola's Back Porch

RESTAURANT/OPERATOR
Lola's Back Porch
New York, NY
YEAR OPENED
1989
DESIGN FIRM
Santi Design
DESIGNERS
Santi Acosta and Lee Stump
ART DIRECTOR
Santi Acosta
PRINTER
William Allen

Lola's Back Porch serves naive America cuisine with a Cajun twist and features Jazz, Gospel, Blues, Reggae, and South American musical entertainment nightly. Located in Manhattan's Flatiron District, the client wanted to incorporate a few of the many 18th and 19th century engravings that hang in the restaurant, into the menu design. Using their existing color scheme of pink and green, the designer created the final results on the MAC IIcx using a Microtek scanner and photoshop software.

Buckeye Roadhouse

RESTAURANT/OPERATOR
Buckeye Roadhouse
Real Restaurants
Mill Valley, CA
YEAR OPENED
1991
DESIGN FIRM
BlackDog
DESIGNER
Mark Fox
ILLUSTRATOR
Mark Fox

Buckeye Roadhouse is a western style eatery serving comfort food. For nearly 55 years, this Marin County restaurant modeled itself after a Teutonic Hunting lodge. Today, only a lone moosehead remains on the premises as a reminder of what the restaurant used to be.

The martini deer with the olive eye logo was inspired by a flashing neon martini glass that restaurateur Bill Higgins wanted to preserve. Over the years it has become something of a mascot. The kinetic exterior signage consists of blinking neon, alternating the stylized deer, the martini glass, and then a composite of the two.

188

BUCKEYE
R O A D H O U S E

BUCKEYE
R O A D H O U S E

In Marin County since 1937, we are just off Highway 101 between Sausalito and Mill Valley. Deluxe Dinners and Cocktails are served nightly. Stop by for our Friday and Weekend Lunches.

BUCK EYE OPENERS

COUNTY MARTINI Bombay Sapphire Gin 94°	4.50
BARBADOS COSMOPOLITAN Mt. Gay Rum, cranberry and lime	4.00
BUCKAROO BONSAI Tequila Kamikaze (from another planet)	4.00
PERFECT NEGRONI Gin, Campari, sweet and dry vermouth	3.75
TAVERN PUNCH Meyers's Rum & orange & pineapple & cranberry & brandy &	4.00
ICED BUCKSHOT Rumple Minze and Jagermeister… Ba Boom!	3.75

APPETIZERS

HOMEMADE SOUP DAILY	3.95
ROASTED EGGPLANT and RED ONION TOAST, tomato vinaigrette	4.95
BLACK FOREST TOSTADA, wild mushrooms, black beans and feta	5.50
ROADHOUSE PIZZA PIE, smoked teleme, asiago, caramelized onions, apple smoked bacon and chard	6.95
ONION RINGS with homemade ketchup	3.95
SMOKED ATLANTIC SALMON with potato leek pancake	6.50
OYSTERS BINGO, broiled with spinach, Ricard and aioli	7.95
GRILLED marinated CHICKEN with Japanese peanut sauce	5.25

SALADS

MIXED GREENS with choice of dressing	4.50
California with smoked almonds	
Bleu cheese and currants	
House vinaigrette	
WARM SPINACH, calamata olives, feta and apple smoked bacon	5.75
SHORELINE, chicory, arugula, endive, figs, pears and bleu cheese	5.50
CAESAR or BRUTUS (with coarse ground chili pepper)	6.95
SMOKED CHICKEN with apples, walnuts, bleu cheese and currants	8.50

SIDES

FRENCH FRIES with homemade ketchup	2.50
GARLIC and CHIVE MASHED POTATOES	1.95
SPICED BLACK BEANS with sour cream and red onions	3.80
PENNSYLVANIA DUTCH COLESLAW	1.95
BUCKEYE BOB'S HOMEMADE PICKLES	1.95
POLENTA	1.95

SANDWICHES

SMOKED TURKEY, avocado, watercress, tomato chutney	6.95
HAMBURGER or CHEESEBURGER, fully garnished	6.50
BARBECUED SLOPPY JOE with chips	6.25
SHRIMP PO-BOY CLUB with old style remoulade	6.95

BUCKWEAR

T-SHIRT awesome with khakis	18.95
SWEATSHIRT classic and comfortable	19.95
HUNTING CAP a must for winter	13.50
TEAM PATCH fancy, iron-on type	3.50

ENTREES

FRESH FISH DAILY	A.Q.
SEAFOOD HASH on leek, mushroom and apple-smoked bacon ragout	11.50
PEPPER and LEMON CREOLE SHRIMP with garlic mashed potatoes	12.95
BARBECUED DUNGENESS CRAB with grilled bread	A.Q.
GRILLED SONOMA RABBIT with basil, garlic and spiced black beans	11.75
HAMMERED CHICKEN CUTLET with red carrots and chard, coarse grain mustard sauce	11.50
SMOKED PETALUMA DUCK with winter fruit chutney	13.75
PORK CHOP with homemade ginger-apple sauce	11.50
BARBECUED BABY BACK RIBS with coleslaw and garlic mashed potatoes	10.95
SAUTEED CALF'S LIVER, homemade chili sauce, bacon and onions	9.75
GRILLED SKIRT STEAK, Tucson tavern marinade and 1937 sauce	12.95
BRAISED LAMB SHANK with shallots, mint and fennel	11.50
BEER SAUSAGES, sweet and sour cabbage, garlic mashed potatoes	9.95

DESSERTS

BAKED LEMON PUDDING with winter fruit	4.50
S'MORE PIE	4.95
CAPPUCCINO CHEESE CAKE	4.95
BUTTERSCOTCH BRULEE	4.50
PUMPKIN PECAN PIE with whipped cream	4.75
CHOCOLATE TOFFEE ICE CREAM SANDWICH	5.50
MILK SHAKES AND MALTEDS	3.00

Stars Lunch and Dinner

RESTAURANT/OPERATOR
**Stars on Hingham Harbor/
Kay's Harbor Corporation
Hingham, MA**
YEAR OPENED
1989
DESIGN FIRM
Marie P. Flaherty Arts and Design
DESIGNER
Marie Flaherty Henderson
ILLUSTRATOR
Marie Flaherty Henderson
PRINTER
Independence Press

The original Stars was based on club car diners, though it has expanded over the years and is now much larger. The design objectives for the new menu included organizing a large amount of items in a relatively small area. The client also wanted to update their colors to reflect the spirit of the restaurant. The brilliant green, hot pink and bright blue used in the menu were also employed in the restaurant's decor. Their intensity duplicates the neon lighting employed in the restaurant's bar. Because the back page is frequently missed, the client wanted a menu that would entice diners to look all the way through. The illustrations were based on styles popular in the '50s. All menus, including take out, the newsletter, coupons and other printed material are consistent in style and include Stars' marvelous sense of humor.

Market Roastery

RESTAURANT/OPERATOR
Market Roastery
San Francisco, CA
YEAR OPENED
1991
DESIGN FIRM
Victoria Rabiner Design
DESIGNER
Victoria Rabiner
PRINTER
Great Impressions

The Market Roastery occupies a large and airy Victorian building in San Francisco. Serving food cooked on an open rotisserie in an American Bistro setting, the client felt a checkered pattern would reflect the restaurant's philosophy of fresh foods at reasonable prices. They wanted a graphics package that would be strong and capture the essence of this bar and restaurant, but a strict budget called for a logo design in black and white. The result was a simple, straightforward menu. The focal point became a flame-like logo surrounded by a plate, wine glass and utensils. The flames are further accentuated, in the business cards, a media invitation and presentation card, by being printed in a bright brick red. Rather than using a checked pattern as a peripheral design element, the checks actually became the logo itself. Each of the four menus, dinner, wine, dessert and cafe, display the same checkered pattern, but use different symbols to identify each particular menu. They are all subdivided by a series of smaller black checks forming a grid.

wine

dessert

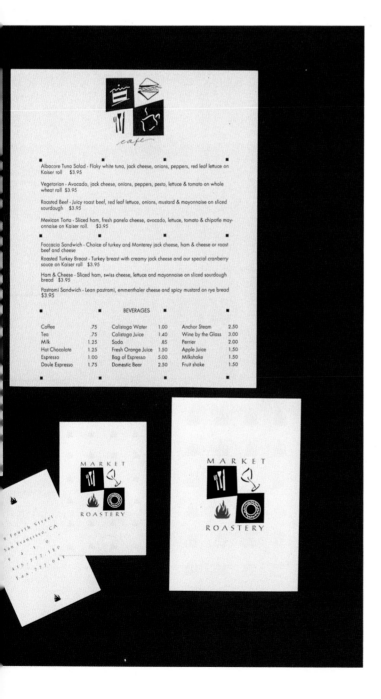

cafe

Cafe Tu Tu Tango

RESTAURANT/OPERATOR
Cafe Tu Tu Tango
Coconut Grove, FL
YEAR OPENED
1991
DESIGN FIRM
Patrick McBride Company
DESIGNER
Raymond Kampf
ILLUSTRATORS
Raymond Kampf and
Alexander Okun
PRINTER
Copy Express

The root of Cafe Tu Tu Tango is an eclectic mix of artwork. Not just contemporary and modern art, but the kind of drawings and paintings that have an artist's insight and perspective. The client wanted the look and feel of an artist's loft; something that would evoke the creativity and persona of a real person. The challenge was to create an environment that was romantic, comfortable and yet would still have the feeling of a studio. Windows from an old industrial building in Chicago were used to impart just the look the owners wanted. Paintings and drawings were supplied by local artists and are in various stages of completion. The decor makes use of paint splattered easels and antiques scrounged from flea markets and garage sales to create an environment that blends beautifully with the internatonal cuisine.

The client needed a menu that would be versatile, one that could easily and quickly incorporate changes with minimal cost. The graphic elements also have an artistic feel, but without being over designed or too trendy. The almost haphazard feel of the surroundings extends to the menus, placemats and other collateral.

CAFÉ TU TU TANGO

ART HAPPY IS TO THE ARTIST AS ORNITHOLOGY IS TO THE BIRDS'

ARTIST DAN COLEN
THE SKY RED - BECAUSE
THEY KNOW IT'S
BLUE
THOSE OF US THAT
AREN'T ARTISTS
MUST COLOR THINGS AS
THEY REALLY ARE, OR
PEOPLE MIGHT THINK
WE'RE STUPID

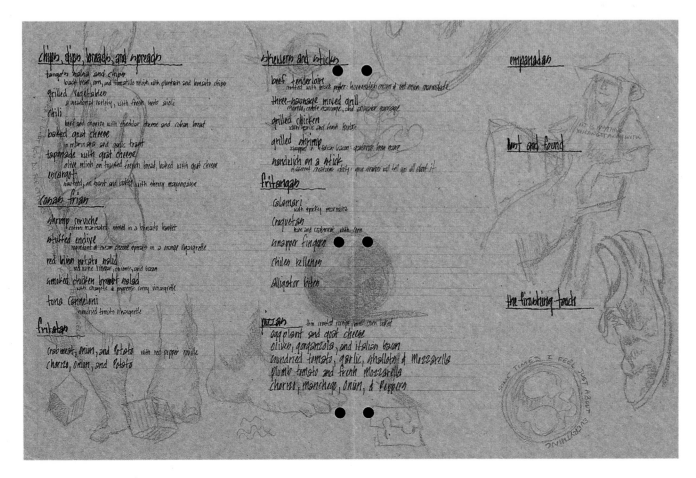

chips, dips, breads, and spreads

tango's salsa and chips
black bean, corn, and tomatillo relish with plantain and bonsito chips

grilled vegetables
a seasonal variety, with fresh herb aioli

chili
beef and chorizo with cheddar cheese and cuban bread

baked goat cheese
in marinara and garlic toast

tapenade with goat cheese
olive relish on toasted french bread, baked with goat cheese

escargot
sautéed, on toast and baked with sherry mayonnaise

cuban frian

shrimp cerviche
citrus marinated, served in a bonsito basket

stuffed endive
roquefort & cream cheese spread in a orange vinaigrette

red bliss potato salad
red wine vinegar, cilantro, and bacon

smoked chicken breast salad
with chayote & peppers curry vinaigrette

tuna canneloni
sundried tomato vinaigrette

fritatas

crab meat, onion, and potato with red pepper rouille
chorizo, onion, and potato

skewers and sticks

beef tenderloin
crusted with black pepper; horseradish cream & red onion marmalade

three-sausage mixed grill
chorizo, creole sausage, and alligator sausage

grilled chicken
with garlic and fresh herbs

grilled shrimp
wrapped in italian bacon - achiote-lime sauce

sandwich on a stick
different mixture daily; your server will tell you all about it

fritangas

calamari
with spicky marinara

croquetas
ham and crabmeat with corn

snapper fingers

chiles rellenos

alligator bites

pizzas thin crusted recipe, wood oven baked

eggplant and goat cheese
olives, gorganzola, and italian bacon
sundried tomato, garlic, shallots & mozzarella
plumb tomato and fresh mozzarella
chorizo, manchego, onion, & peppers

empanadas

lost and found

the finishing touch

SOME TIMES I FEEL JUST ABOUT EVERYTHING

ART IS ANYTHING YOU CAN GET AWAY WITH

CHAPTER

12

Kids

Bennigan's Book/Placemat

RESTAURANT/OPERATOR
Bennigan's/S & A Corporation
Dallas, TX
YEAR OPENED
1967
DESIGN FIRM
Baker & Grooms
DESIGNER
Mikie Baker
ILLUSTRATOR
The Creative Group
PRINTER
Allcraft

At Bennigan's, the children's menu selections are presented in a placemat format with a game board that teaches and encourages recycling. It complements this chain restaurant's creative treatment of children. By improvising with coins and crayons it can actually be played and serves as a tool for learning. The back of the menu can be used for coloring. The hope is that children will be occupied while waiting for their meal and then take the placemat/menu home as a reminder of the fun they had at the restaurant. The activities book can also be used for coloring and serves as an interesting diversion for children. It offers much in the way of tabletop entertainment and is updated every six weeks. Bennigan's also offers all children's meals served in a plastic dump truck, a particularly popular option.

KINGSWAY

For Children 10 & Under

Hamburger
Includes golden French Fries

Grilled Cheese
Includes Potato Chips

Spaghetti
Jr. Portion served with Meat Sauce

French Toast
With Butter and Syrup

Fish & Chips
Served with French Fries

Boneless Chicken Nuggets
Served with French Fries

Pancakes
Three Kingsway Pancakes and One Egg, any style

Bacon, Egg, & Toast
Two Strips of Bacon, One Egg any style, and Toast.

Kingsway Family Restaurant

RESTAURANT/OPERATOR
Kingsway Family Restaurant
DESIGN FIRM
A.D. Paustian Design
DESIGNER
Anthony Paustian
ART DIRECTOR
Anthony Paustian
ILLUSTRATOR
Christopher Boyd

Being a family restaurant, Kingsway has mass appeal with good food at low prices. However, the restaurant needed something that would distinguish it from other nearby family restaurants. Perhaps the most innovative feature of the children's menu is that is offers children and adults an opportunity to familiarize themselves with sign language. It is an interesting diversion for the children and a great way to stimulate conversation. The designer, Anthony Paustian, used illustrations, by artist Christopher Boyd. On the cover of the children's menu, a child is handing a knight his shield. The regular breakfast and dinner menus are each a variation on this same knight theme. The prices on all three are done in calligraphy, a bow to the piece's medieval styling.

Dino Fun

PROJECT
Kenyon Generic Menus
DESIGN FIRM
Kenyon Press
DESIGNER
Richard Witt
ILLUSTRATOR
Robert Greisen
PRINTER
Kenyon Press

Kenyon Press wanted to create a children's menu that would not only be entertaining, but colorful, attractive and capture the imagination of children too. A series of six different dinosaurs were custom printed with four-color illustrations. To help occupy their time while at the table, different games, riddles and activities are offered with each piece. There is also explanatory text about each of the six featured dinosaurs that familiarizes children with the pronunciation of the name and teaches them something about these extinct creatures. Die-cut, these menus have bottom flaps that interconnect so they can act as table tents when desired.

Willie C's Kid's Menu

RESTAURANT/OPERATOR
Willie C's Cafe & Bar
Wichita, KS
DESIGN FIRM
Blick Benest and Company
DESIGNER
Gary Benest
ILLUSTRATOR
Gary Benest
PRINTER
Quality Printing

Designed to duplicate the look of a West-Texas cafe, Willie C's is authentic right down to the lunch counter. These menus were primarily developed to assist children and encourage them to identify with the restaurant. The designer, Gary Benest, developed this budget-conscious piece to portray the friendly, casual atmosphere. Printed in two-color on a plain white paper stock, it can be saved and used again, taken home as a souvenir, or when it becomes soiled, simply thrown away.

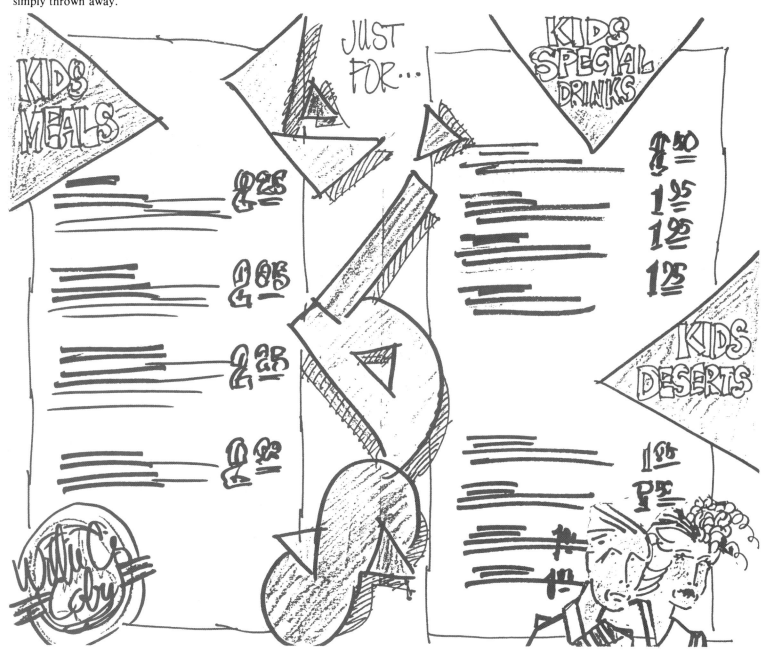

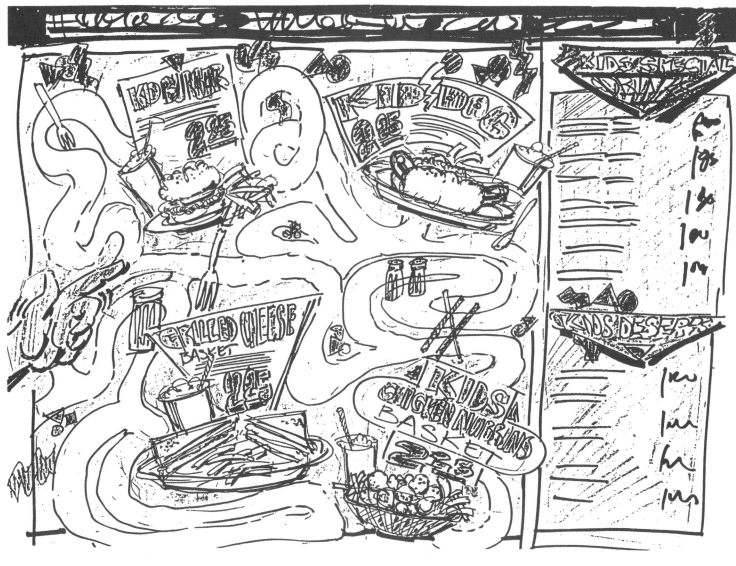

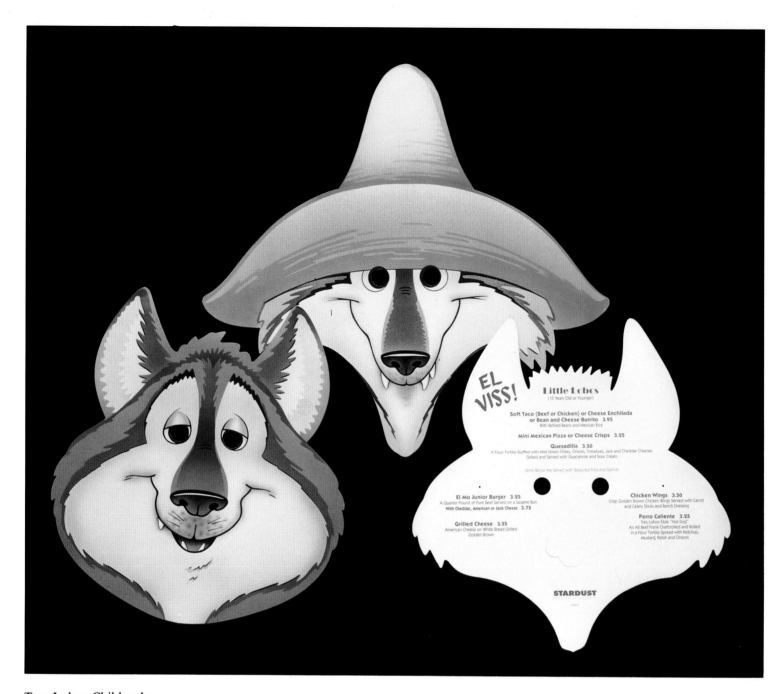

Tres Lobos Children's Menu and Survival Kit

RESTAURANT/OPERATOR
Tres Lobos
Stardust Resort and Casino
Las Vegas, NV
DESIGN FIRM
Kenyon Press
DESIGNER
Richard Witt
ILLUSTRATOR
Richard Witt
PRINTER
Kenyon Press

Tres Lobos is a fun restaurant featuring Mexican food in a casual atmosphere. The name, meaning three wolves in Spanish, is in honor of the key executives of the Boyd group in Las Vegas. This series of three menus was developed by designer Richard Witt as a way to entertain children and give them a souvenir to take with them. It becomes a toy too, something they can play with that will remind them of the fun they had at Los Lobos.

Lyon's Restaurant

RESTAURANT/OPERATOR
Lyon's Restaurant
Foster City, CA
YEAR OPENED
1962
DESIGN FIRM
Marriott and Asay
DESIGNER
Alfred Lediard
ILLUSTRATOR
Alfred Lediard
PRINTER
Sun Litho

The challenge with these placemat designs was to create something for children that would be fun and involving. The client wanted a menu that would aid in making their restaurant, Lyon's, located in Foster City, California, more appealing to children. Their aim was to find a way to keep kids occupied so parents could enjoy a cocktail before dinner.

Salle a Manager

RESTAURANT/OPERATOR
Salle a Manager/Grand Hotel
Mackinac Island, MI
YEAR OPENED
1887
DESIGN FIRM
Reeser Advertising Associates
DESIGNER
Nancy C. Reeser
ART DIRECTOR
Nancy C. Reeser
ILLUSTRATOR
Robin Agnew
PRINTER
Thomas Printing

The Grand Hotel on Mackinac Island wanted to create a special menu for young ladies and gentlemen in a clear, easy-to-read format that would be cost effective. The presentation had to have as much appeal to adults as it would to children. The renderings of a boy and girl are reminiscent of old children's book illustrations. The colors chosen and the design treatment on the front and back of the menus correlate to the main dining room's decor.

Red Robin's Kids

RESTAURANT/OPERATOR
Red Robin
South Sound Red Robin Franchise
Seattle, WA
YEAR OPENED
1982
DESIGN FIRM
South Sound Red Robin (in house)
DESIGNER
Jim Roths
PRINTER
Graphic Services

This fun-filled menu designed by Jim Roths gives children the opportunity to order by picture. Each of the food selections has a playful name and is illustrated as a cartoon character. It helps to make the Red Robin dining experience fun for children.

This menu was a 1991 NRA Second Place winner in the "Specialty" category.

Stars Children's

RESTAURANT/OPERATOR
Stars on Hingham Harbor/
Kay's Harbor Corporation
Hingham, MA
YEAR OPENED
1989
DESIGN FIRM
Marie P. Flaherty Arts and Design
DESIGNER
Marie Flaherty Henderson
ILLUSTRATOR
Marie Flaherty Henderson
PRINTER
Independence Press

At Stars, the design objective was to update colors to reflect the spirit of the restaurant. The space was taken over after a former eatery had failed, so the owners wanted to redesign for a new look. The original restaurant was based on club car diners and Stars has maintained this concept, but expanded the restaurant's space.

Like their regular menu, the illustrations for the children's menu were based on some old '50s graphics. Changing the headings to a crayon style makes this piece an exciting and appealing one for the younger set and delineates it from the regular menu. The colors mirror the other menu and duplicate those used in the restaurant's interior. All menus including the take-out, newsletters, coupons and other printed collateral work through color, typeface, formatting and Stars' sense of humor.

Children's Menu

Breakfast

two pancakes	1.95
w/meat	2.50
cereal	1.25
fruit loops, cheerios	
child's french toast	1.95
w/meat	2.50

Lunch/Dinner

pasta	3.95
w/homemade tomato sauce	
homemade chicken fingers	3.95
chicken wings	3.95
grilled cheese	2.50
w/tomato	2.75
w/bacon & tomato	3.00
tuna fish sandwich	2.95
chicken salad sandwich	3.25
6" boboli pizza	
cheese	3.50
pepperoni	3.95
sausage	3.95
pepper & onion	3.95
canadian bacon	3.95
vegetable	3.95

all of the above Lunch and Dinner entrees are prepared with lots of love. all items come served with fries except for the pizza and the pasta.

Desserts

jr. hot fudge sundae	1.95
ice cream	1.25
jr. strawberry shortcake	1.95

this menu is for children only. proper i.d. not required. we hope you enjoy **STARS.**

CHAPTER

13

South of the Border

Acapulco Dinner Menu

RESTAURANT/OPERATOR
**Acapulco Restaurant
Long Beach, CA**
YEAR OPENED
1960
DESIGN FIRM
Partners By Design
DESIGNER
Jeff Courtney
PHOTOGRAPHER
Burke/Triolo Studios
PRINTER
Color Graphics

Acapulco began operation in 1960 and is now a California chain with 50 restaurants. The color palette and menu graphics are in harmony with the newly renovated restaurant interior, as well as with the exterior and signage elements.

The theme, "The Art Of Mexican Cooking," is carried throughout the menu. Photography was extensively utilized to visually identify sections and increase appetite appeal. The piece includes photo vignettes and descriptions of some of the more unique and distinctive ingredients, including the spices and salsas used in the preparation of Acapulco's authentic dishes. Bright graphics break up the visual relief from the regular menu. Each sidebar correlates to a specific ingredient and the dishes listed beneath it make use of that particular food item.

Tortilla Flats

RESTAURANT/OPERATOR
Tortilla Flats
San Luis Obispo, CA
YEAR OPENED
1974
DESIGN FIRM
DCO Design Communications
DESIGNER
James Wigger
ART DIRECTOR
Matt Thulé
ILLUSTRATORS
James Wigger and Matt Thulé
PRINTER
Central Coast Printing

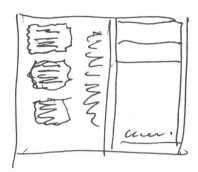

Tortilla Flats is housed in a rustic turn-of-the-century brick creamery. The client wanted a festive menu for their Southwestern style cuisine, and requested a piece that would present the selections in a simple and easy-to-read fashion. To accomplish this with such an extensive menu, each selection was given a number that includes its Spanish translation. Some of the numbers take on visual characteristics, such as the number "4" designed to look like a saguaro cactus. The user-friendly text and lively layout make this menu a pleasure to read. A flecked recycled paper was chosen because it has the texture of a tortilla chip.

S DE LA CASA
SALAD WITH BELOW ITEMS ADD .95

VOCADO CON CAMARONES
Fresh avocado half, piled high with
shrimp sauteed in verde sauce and
topped with cheese. Served with a
cheese enchilada, rice, Cuban style
black beans and tortillas. $10.95

CHILE RELLENOS DE CAMARONES
Two freshly roasted and peeled
Anaheim chiles stuffed with jack
cheese and shrimp, dipped in a light
batter and fried golden. Topped with
verde sauce. Served with rice and
Cuban style black beans. $9.95

TAQUITOS (4)
Crispy rolled corn tortillas filled with
shredded beef, bell pepper and onions.
Served with guacamole, rice and
refried beans. $6.95

HICKEN FLAUTAS (3)
Flour tortillas rolled and packed with
chicken and fried to a golden brown.
Rice and refried beans too! $6.95

TRES AMIGOS
Three enchiladas—one shrimp, one
chicken and one cheese, each dressed
in a different sauce and served with
rice and Cuban style black beans.
What a taste adventure! $8.95

TRO

CIALTIES

CHICKEN FAJITAS
Marinated chicken in a spicy mixture
of seasonings and combined with
onions, tomatoes and bell peppers in
a sizzling skillet. Top this off with
rice, Cuban style black beans, pico de
gallo, guacamole and sour cream. Hot
flour tortillas to roll your own! $8.95

CARNITAS
Cubes of seasoned pork, deep fried
and served with sauteed onions,
tomatoes and bell peppers in a sizzling skillet. Served with rice, refried
beans, guacamole, sour cream, pico
de gallo, and hot flour tortillas. $8.95

ENCHILADAS Y BURRITOS
SERVED WITH RICE & BEANS

BURRITO COLORADO
Our own Chile Colorado and beans
rolled in a flour tortilla and covered
with enchilada sauce. $6.95

CHILE VERDE BURRITO
Tender morsels of pork in a verde
sauce with beans, rolled in a flour
tortilla. Topped with verde sauce and
garnished with sour cream. $6.95

BURRITO DE POLLO
Tender pieces of chicken with beans
rolled in a flour tortilla covered with
enchilada sauce and sour cream
garnish. $6.25

BURRITO ESPECIAL
Shredded beef and beans rolled in a
flour tortilla topped with ranchera
sauce and sour cream garnish. $6.25

BEAN & CHEESE BURRITO $4.95

CRAB ENCHILADAS
Enchiladas stuffed with crab and
cheese, covered with our subtly spicy
verde sauce and topped with sour
cream. $8.95

SHRIMP ENCHILADAS
A delicious combination of shrimp,
tomatoes and cilantro covered with
verde sauce and garnished with sour
cream. $8.95

ENCHILADA TORTA
A triple decker enchilada layered
with chicken, cheese, and topped with
ranchera sauce. Served with rice. $6.95

ENCHILADAS VERDES
Two chicken enchiladas covered
with verde sauce, melted cheese and
sour cream. $6.95

ENCHILADAS RANCHERAS
Two cheese enchiladas smothered in
ranchera sauce. $6.95

We accept MasterCard, VISA, and American Express.
No personal checks, please.

ENTREMESES (appetizers)

GUACAMOLE
avocado, tomato, onions, jalapeño chiles, cilantro and lemon 5.25

SOPES SURTIDOS
two crisp corn tortillas filled with pork and adobo sauce 4.95
two crisp corn tortillas filled with shrimp and chipotle sauce 5.50
two crisp corn tortillas filled with black beans, cactus strips and fresh cheese 4.25

QUESADILLAS SURTIDAS
three corn tortilla turnovers filled with cheese and potato, mushrooms, zucchini 5.95

CHALUPAS CON POLLO Y CREMA
crisp corn tortilla boats topped with marinated chicken breast, jalapeño chiles, cream and fresh cheese 4.50

TAMALITOS SURTIDOS
little tamales - fresh corn masa stuffed with chicken and pumpkin seed sauce; pork with guajillo chile sauce 4.95

CEVICHE DE PESCADO Y CAMARONES
fresh fish and shrimp marinated in lime and lemon juices with chopped onions, tomato, jalapeño chiles, cilantro and avocado Grande 6.50   Chica 4.50

CAMARONES CON SALSA DE AGUACATE Y TEQUILA
cold poached shrimp with avocado-tequila dressing

TRIBILIN "GOOFY"
marinated fresh fish and

PLATI

TAMALES (stuffed fresh corn masa)

TAMALES DE PECHUGA DE POLLO
two tamales of chicken with green and red chile sauces; served in a corn husk 8.50

TAMALES DE MASA A LA OAXAQUENA
two tamales of pork with guajillo chile sauce; served in banana leaves 8.25

TAMALES DE ELOTE CON NOPALES Y PLATANO
green corn masa stuffed with cactus and plantain; steamed in green corn husk 8.50

PLATILLO DE TAMALES SURTIDOS
an assortment of three tamales, one of each of the above 10.50

PLATILLOS FAVORITOS (Mexican favorites)

POLLO EN MOLE
double breast of chicken with sauce of chocolate, chiles, fruits and spices 10.95

CARNITAS URUAPAN
slowly-roasted pork sirloin, onions, cilantro and serrano chiles 10.50

PATO DE GRANJA EN PIPIAN
roasted duck with pumpkin seed sauce 12.95

POLLO CON ACHIOTE Y NOPALES
marinated chicken breast with cactus strips and onions; served in a molcajete 10.95

POZOLE TRES AMIGOS
corn kernels, black beans, poblano rice, pork, chicken, avocado, tortilla strips, served with radishes, lettuce and lemon 8.95

FILETE DE CERDO CON PIÑA
pork tenderloin with adobo sauce and grilled pineapple 11.95

CARNE CON CEBOLLITAS
marinated skirt steak with onions and cilantro dressing; served on a sizzling platter 11.50

CAMARONES AL TAMARINDO
sautéed shrimp with tomatillos and chipotle-tamarind sauce 14.50

CALDO DE MARISCOS
seafood broth with clams, shrimp, mussels, fish and squid 10.50

• SERVED WITH HOT TORTILLAS, BLACK BEANS AND FIDEO •

A LA PARILLA (mesquite charcoal grilled)

PESCADO DEL DIA
fresh fish served with sautéed seasonal vegetables and chipotle-cilantro butter A.Q.

CAMARONES A LA SAL DE ROCA
giant shrimp cooked over rock salt with cilantro-jalapeño dressing 15.95

TAMPIQUEÑA ELOTE ASADO
marinated top sirloin steak with sautéed onions, pasilla peppers, mushrooms and grilled corn 12.75

ROSTISADA DEL DIA
spit-roasted meats and fowl (daily selection) A.Q.

LONGANIZA CON SALSA VERDE Y ROJA
grilled homemade sausage served with green and red salsas 9.50

DON CACAHUATE
double breast of chicken with peanut-serrano chile sauce 10.95

PLATILLO DE MARISCOS FRESCOS SURTIDOS
large platter of assorted fresh seafood (for two or more) A.Q.

• SERVED WITH HOT TORTILLAS, BLACK BEANS AND FIDEO •

¡Salud!

¡Salud!

RESTAURANT/OPERATOR
¡Salud!/Spectrum Foods
San Francisco, CA
YEAR OPENED
1991
DESIGN FIRM
The Thompson Design Group
DESIGNER
Jody & Dennis Thompson
ART DIRECTOR
Lisa Sanford
PRINTER
Pacific Lithograph Company

The interior of ¡Salud!, in San Francisco, is primarily white with beautiful multi-colored murals, custom brass light fixtures and stair banisters, and with a long curving copper bar. The distressed steel and water buffalo-hide chairs and stone inlaid tables make the bar the most popular room in the restaurant.

By using copper foil, the menus correspond to the extensive use of copper in Salud's dining room. The leather thong ties and tactile stock enhance the authentic feel, while creating a distinctive look that reinforces the upscale focus of this authentic Mexican restaurant.

The design package creates an inviting ''Mexican'' appeal that is just as comfortable for the black-tie set going to the opera across the street as it is for the blue jean crowd visiting the nearby Museum of Modern Art.

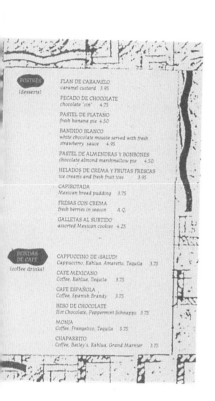

Carlita's Mexican Restaurant

RESTAURANT/OPERATOR
**Carlita's Mexican Restaurant/
Zim's Restaurants
Hayward, CA**
YEAR OPENED
1991-remodel
DESIGN FIRM
BlackDog
DESIGNER
Mark Fox
ILLUSTRATOR
Mark Fox
PRINTER
**Techni-Graphics and
ACME Silkscreen**

Because of the recent remodeling, it became evident that Carlita's needed to upgrade their graphics. Designer Mark Fox created a logo that is an adaptation of an ancient Mexican motif. The menu cover is a synthetic material called Buckskin, which has a leather-like quality that is enriched with age. It tends to be extremely durable, and works well with silkscreening. The choice of Copperplate as the menu's interior typestyle presents the food sections in a clean and legible manner that is fun to read. The raffia tie lends a note of hand-made quality to the overall menu design and works to secure the insert pages.

Carlita's

Especialidades de Carlita

Fajitas

FAJITAS AL CARBON
STRIPS OF MARINATED BEEF OR CHICKEN, OR A COMBINATION
OF BOTH, GRILLED AND SERVED ON A SIZZLING PLATTER
WITH ONIONS AND BELL PEPPERS.................................. 9.95

FAJITAS GRANDE
A DOUBLE ORDER FOR TWO.................................. 18.95

SERVED WITH RICE, REFRIED BEANS, GUACAMOLE, LETTUCE,
SOUR CREAM, TAQUITO MIX AND TORTILLAS.

CHILE RELLENO POBLANO
FRESH POBLANO CHILE FILLED WITH JACK CHEESE,
DIPPED IN A BEER BATTER AND TOPPED WITH FRESH RANCHERA SALSA........ 7.25

POLLO CON CHABACANO
BREAST OF CHICKEN WITH MARINATED RAISINS, APRICOTS AND ALMONDS
SERVED IN A APRICOT CREAM SAUCE. ACCOMPANIED WITH COCONUT-SPANISH
RICE AND FRESH SEASONAL VEGETABLES........................... 8.95

BANDERILLA DE AL CARBON
GRILLED BEEF OR CHICKEN SERVED IN A BROCHETTE STYLE,
ON COCONUT-SPANISH RICE WITH BLACK BEANS...................... 9.50

CARNE A LA BRAZAS (BBQ BABY BACK RIBS)
BASTED IN A HOMEMADE SAUCE AND GRILLED OVER AN OPEN FIRE
SERVED WITH RED POTATOES AND SEASONAL VEGETABLES.............. 9.50

POLLO CON ALCACHOFA
GRILLED BONELESS BREAST OF CHICKEN WITH ARTICHOKE BOTTOMS IN A
SALSA TROPICALE, SERVED WITH BLACK BEANS AND SEASONAL VEGETABLES.... 8.95

CARNE ADOBADAS
A HOUSE-SMOKED CENTER CUT PORK CHOP, SEASONED AND TOPPED WITH A
PEACH CITRUS CHUTNEY AND SERVED WITH RED POTATOES AND SEASONAL
VEGETABLES.. 9.50

CAMARONES CON QUESO
SAUTEED BUTTERFLIED PRAWNS TOSSED IN A JALAPENO CHEESE AND
SPINACH SAUCE, SERVED WITH RICE AND BLACK BEANS................10.95

SNAPPER TROPICALE
SERVED OVER A BLACK BEAN SAUCE, TOPPED WITH CHILI JICAMA RELISH AND
ACCOMPANIED BY COCONUT-SPANISH RICE AND SEASONAL VEGETABLES....... 8.95

SOUTHWESTERN ROLL
MARINATED GRILLED CHICKEN WITH BELL PEPPERS, SNOW PEAS, BLACK BEANS
AND SPINACH ROLLED IN A WHOLE WHEAT TORTILLA................... 8.95

CAMARONES CHILE RELLENO
TENDER BAY SHRIMP AND GUACAMOLE IN A FRESH POBLANO CHILE,
SERVE WITH A POMEGRANATE SAUCE............................... 8.50

Platillos Tradicionales

CHILE VERDE
LEAN PORK SIMMERED IN SALSA VERDE AND GREEN TOMATILLOS............ 7.95

CARNITAS
TENDER PORK, SLOWLY SIMMERED
SERVED WITH TOMATILLO AND RANCHERA SALSAS, AND FLOUR TORTILLAS.... 7.95

ENCHILADAS CANCUN
TWO ENCHILADAS FILLED WITH CRAB, PRAWNS AND SHRIMP
IN A LIGHT CHEESE SAUCE...................................... 8.95

BURRITO SUPREMO
A GIANT FLOUR TORTILLA FILLED WITH SHREDDED BEEF, CHICKEN,
RICE AND BEANS TOPPED WITH SALSA VERDE AND CHEESE................ 8.95

ENCHILADAS
YOUR CHOICE OF CHEESE, SEASONED CHICKEN, BEEF OR CHILE VERDE........ 5.95

TACOS
SEASONED CHICKEN OR BEEF
ON A CRISP CORN OR SOFT FLOUR TORTILLA........................ 5.50

BURRITO
CHOICE OF EITHER CHICKEN, BEEF OR CHILE VERDE
WRAPPED IN OUR FRESH TORTILLA................................ 6.50

CHIMICHANGA
YOUR CHOICE OF CHICKEN, BEEF OR CHILE VERDE.................... 6.50

FLAUTAS
CRISP GOLDEN CORN TORTILLAS FILLED WITH CHICKEN OR BEEF........... 5.50

TAMALE
PORK OR CHICKEN FILLED CORN MASA IN THE HUSK.................. 5.95

Platillo Gordo de Carlita

THIS COMBINATION INCLUDES YOUR CHOICE OF BEEF, CHICKEN OR CHEESE
ENCHILADA, BEEF OR CHICKEN TACO, PLUS AN ORDER OF BEEF AND CHICKEN
FAJITAS WITH FLOUR TORTILLAS.................... 2 COMPADRES FOR 18.95

Combinaciones

BURRITO Y ENCHILADA
BEEF OR CHICKEN BURRITO AND A CHEESE, CHICKEN OR BEEF ENCHILADA..... 8.50

TACO Y ENCHILADA
BEEF OR CHICKEN TACO AND CHEESE, CHICKEN OR BEEF ENCHILADA......... 8.50

La Cazuela

RESTAURANT/OPERATOR
La Cazuela
Northampton, MA
YEAR OPENED
1984
DESIGN FIRM
in house
ART DIRECTOR/DESIGNER
Barry Steeves
PRINTER
Gazette Printing

The cover of La Cazuela's menu is a slightly surrealistic juxtaposition of the desert landscape with various design elements from the restaurant. The drawing on the wall resembles the restaurant's interior. A large earthenware cooking pot, or cazuela, is in the foreground. It is from this the restaurant derived its name. The ziggurat or stepped pyramid is a motif associated with both Mexican culture and Southwestern Indian art. It is used throughout La Cazuela and in all the restaurant's graphics; all design elements are characteristic of the Southwestern theme. The images of the cazuela and ziggurat are found on matchbooks, signs, print advertising and promotional merchandise such as t-shirts and coffee mugs.

Inside, the main body of the menu is presented in a crisp, clean, easy-to-read format that repeats the cazuela and ziggurat motifs established by the cover. The light flecked pattern that characterizes this recycled paper is nicely employed to complement the desert landscape theme.

La Pinata

RESTAURANT/OPERATOR
La Pinata
Tom Duffy
Burlingame, CA
YEAR OPENED
1982
DESIGN FIRM
Bruce Yelaska Design
DESIGNER
Bruce Yelaska
PRINTER
Vision Printing

La Pinata is a Mexican bar and restaurant that re-creates a festive environment. Part of the decor includes two live parrots. The parrot developed for the logo has a fun, graphic look to express the restaurant's lively atmosphere. It is also integrated into the typography so naturally that the tilde for the letter "N" easily looks like the parrot's foot. The letter "N," slightly dropped as though falling from a pinata, adds a festive touch as well.

LA PIÑATA

LA PIÑATA

LA PIÑATA

LA PIÑATA

LA PIÑATA

1205 BURLINGAME AVE   BURLINGAME, CA 94010

415-375-1070

RESTAURANT
& BAR

HACIENDA

SOUTH OF TH

MARGARITA:
Try our famous traditional or strawberry Margaritas. By the regular or jumbo glass, or for the thirstier crew, by the pitcher.
Strawberry................ $ 2.75 Regular...$ 2.50
Strawberry Jumbo.... 3.25 Jumbo...... 3.00
Strawberry Pitcher.... 12.00 Pitcher.... 10.00

MARGARITA GRANDE:
The Hacienda's Ultimate Margarita Jose Cuervo Gold Tequila & Cointreau...................3.50

CACTUS COOLER:
This refreshing fruit drink has everything it takes to cool you down.
...................2.75

BAD BURRO:
This drink kicks back! A delicious blend of two fruit juices and three liquors...................2.75

POCO LOCO:
"A little bit crazy" if you are ready to let loose. Excellent at the end of a long day ... or, to start off a "crazy" weekend!...................2.75

PINA COLADA:
Delightfully soothing and satisfying. A creamy blend of pineapple, coconut and rum......2.50

PINATA SURPRISE:
A delicious strawberry drink full of sweet surprises...................

TEQUILA SUNRISE:
A drink to enjoy any time of the day. The sun rises before your eyes...................2.75

TEQUILA SUNSET:
The perfect way to enjoy the end of a day. Orange juice and Blackberry Brandy are combined for your very own sunset...................2.75

BEERS:

Draft................... glass pitcher
.... $1.00 $4.75
Ask your Waitress for your Favorite Mexican-Imported or Domestic Bottled BEER!

Tr
speci
meal"
or wita
your er

KEOKE
Dark Cr
to give y

CAFE de
Tequila, Kai

TIA MARIA
Tia Maria and

CAFE MARN
Grand Marnier

SIMPATICO C
A pleasant combi
Creme de Cocoa-tw
a cup of coffee...

All coffee drinks top

Hacienda

RESTAURANT/OPERATOR
Hacienda
Wilkes-Barre, PA
YEAR OPENED
1991
DESIGN FIRM
Jennings Design Associates
DESIGNER
Bruce Jennings
ART DIRECTOR
Ron Stark
PRINTER
Kisel

The challenge for Hacienda was to upgrade the "Mexican" design for the decor of both an operating restaurant and a new one about to open. The owners did not want the sombrero or donkey motifs, so cliché and typically associated with Mexican restaurants. The design integrates earth colors with historic illustrations on an earthy paper stock that helps to convey the natural ingredients used in the restaurant's kitchen.

Tijuana On Fire

RESTAURANT/OPERATOR
Tijuana On Fire
Westminster, CA
DESIGN FIRM
On The Edge
DESIGNER
Jeff Gasper
ART DIRECTOR
Joe Mozdzen
ILLUSTRATOR
Jeff Gasper
PRINTER
Sand Graphics

Tijuana On Fire, is a fast food restaurant located in The Westminster Mall food court. The restaurant and its identity borrow from the rich warm tones and textures of Mexico. Bringing Mexican food to a Southern California audience, Tijuana On Fire insists on using only fresh ingredients. They make their own salsa daily, use real sour cream, fresh produce and even feature tacos made with fish.

The designer, Jeff Gasper, created a small menu that is unpretentious but fun. Using recycled stock for all their promotions, packaging and identity, Tijuana On Fire is big on creating "Corporate Culture" with a conscience.

THE BEST
FROM
MEXICO

Westminster Mall
Food Court
Westminster, CA 92683
(714) 373-2257

TIJUANA'S BEST

Your Choice of Chicken, Steak or Carnitas

Taco Grande	
corn tortillas, avocado, beans, salsa & cilantro	1.95
Burrito Tijuana	
flour tortilla, cheese, guacamole, sour cream & salsa	2.75
Torta	
french roll, sour cream, guacamole, mayonnaise, lettuce, tomatoes & bell peppers	2.75
Tostada Tijuana	
black beans, lettuce, mild salsa, guacamole, sour cream, cheese & chips	4.25
Ensalada de Pollo	
all Mexican greens, lettuce, bell peppers, tomatoes, avocados and cheese	4.50
Quesadilla	
flour tortilla with cheese & guacamole	1.95
Quesadilla with Meat	
chicken, steak or carnitas.	2.95
Nachos	
regular and blue chips, beans, mild salsa, cheese, sour cream, guacamole & chives	3.50
Nachos with meat	4.50

BUENOS DIAS TIJUANA!

Breakfast
Coffee Included
Served Until 11:30 am

Breakfast Burrito	
scrambled eggs, salsa, cheese & meat	2.25
Breakfast Taco	
scrambled eggs, salsa & meat on corn tortillas	1.25
Omelette Tijuana	
cheese, avocado, salsa & meat	2.50
with rice , beans & tortillas	3.50
Huevos Rancheros	
fried eggs, sour cream, guacamole, salsa, rice, beans & tortillas	3.50
Huevos a la Mexicana	
eggs and salsa mixed with rice, beans & tortillas	3.50

SIDE ORDERS

Black Beans	.95
Rice	.95
Chips	1.25
Guacamole	.85
Sour Cream	.50
Tortillas	.50
Salsa to go 8 oz.	1.50

BEVERAGES

	S	M	L
Coke, Sprite, Diet Coke, Dr. Pepper	.60	.75	.90
Horchata, Jamaica, Pina, Ice Tea	.60	.75	.90
Caramba, Penafiel			1.00
Coffee, Milk			.60

Border Grill

RESTAURANT/OPERATOR
Border Grill/l.a. Eyeworks, Inc.
Los Angeles, CA
DESIGN FIRM
l.a. Eyeworks inhouse design
DESIGNER
Menu: Mike Fink
ART DIRECTOR
Gai Gherardi
ILLUSTRATORS
Su Huntley and Donna Muir

The Border Grill has two locations, one in downtown Santa Monica and the original on Melrose Avenue in Los Angeles. The interior of Border Grill is dominated by the bold, animated murals of two London artists, Su Huntley and Donna Muir. This popular Cal-Mex restaurant interprets a colorful, South-of-the-Border carnival atmosphere. It represents a distinctive aesthetic, one with universal appeal that is slightly skewed, but highly original. The artists were trying to reproduce something of the look and feel of the street graffiti found in Mexico. They used traditional elements such as the devil and giant demons for authenticity.

The menus are strikingly rendered in black and white. The art director on the project, Gai Gherardi, had total freedom and didn't need to work around any of the restaurant's elements.

The type style and general layout were done by graphic designer Mike Fink. The menu was done as a collaboration between Gherardi, Fink and the two artists.

CHAPTER
14

Flexible Formats

Susie Kate's

RESTAURANT/OPERATOR
Susie Kate's
San Francisco, CA
YEAR OPENED
1987
DESIGN FIRM
Jim Hurd Design
DESIGNER
Charles Low
ART DIRECTOR
Jim Hurd
ILLUSTRATOR
Jim Hurd

Susie Kate's in San Francisco is a traditional restaurant offering Southern fare. The menu's graphics are representative of the restaurant's picnic styled interior. The designer, Charles Low, made use of his Macintosh, a laser printer and a color copier to produce a flexible color menu at a reasonable cost. The text is printed on an acetate sheet and overlays a print of the color art. The two pages can then be inserted into a conventional plastic menu holder. The menu overlays can be updated as needed and laser-printed independent of the color sheet. Goudy, with its beautiful traditional letter-forms, was chosen as the typeface.

Eulipia

RESTAURANT/OPERATOR
Eulipia-Restaurant & Bar
San Jose, CA
YEAR OPENED
1980
DESIGN FIRM
(?Paradox!)
DESIGNER
Alfredo Muccino
PHOTOGRAPHER
Franklin Avery
PRINTER
Rosicrucian Press

Uncomplicated, colorful, and amusing are all words used to describe the mood created with furnishings and wall treatments at this restaurant in San Jose, California. Choosing a small format and primary colors for the menu covers adds a dimension of fun and brightness to Eulipia's already lively atmosphere. Designer Alfredo Muccino says, "the playfulness of the typography is visually exciting while not compromising legibility." Utilizing state-of-the-art technology, the designer developed the logo and menu design on the Macintosh, thus eliminating the need to make conventional comps and thumbnails. The bright covers are simply a logo sticker affixed to colored paper.

Piemonte Ovest

RESTAURANT/OPERATOR
Piemonte Ovest
Oakland, CA
YEAR OPENED
1991
DESIGN FIRM
Judi Radice Design Consultant
DESIGNER
Cary Trout
ART DIRECTOR
Judi Radice
ILLUSTRATOR
Hand-lettering by Cary Trout
PHOTOGRAPHER
Beatriz Coll
PRINTER
On Paper

Piemonte Ovest, located on the Piedmont/Oakland border in Northern California, serves food influenced by the cultures and cuisines of the Mediterranean. Upon entering the restaurant, housed in a Victorian era building, there is an immediate feeling of warmth. The goal of the menu design was to complement that mood of cordiality and to offer customers an attractive presentation. Since the restaurant was new, the chef needed to be able to refine the menu, hence the evolution of the letterhead design. The borders are reproductions of the marble used on the bar and table tops. A slab of the stone was copied on a color laser copier, and then made into two pieces of film by the printer.

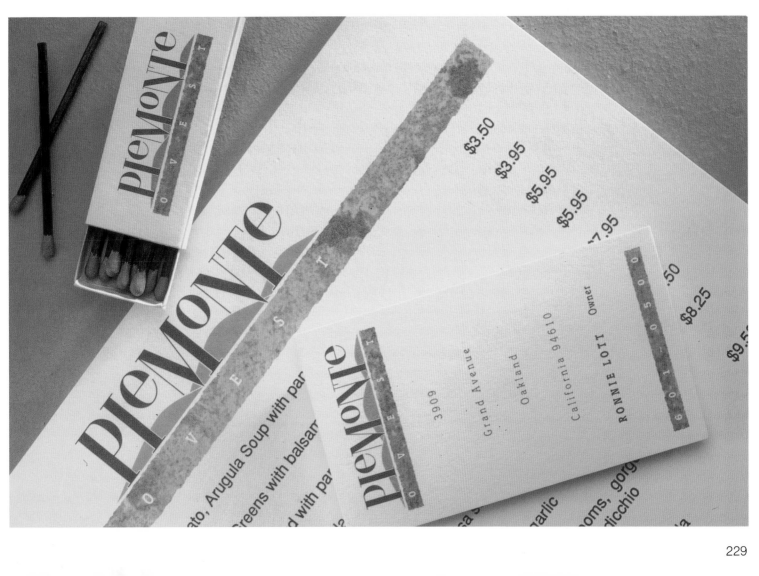

Postrio

RESTAURANT/OPERATOR
Postrio Restaurant
Kimco Hotel Management
San Francisco, CA
YEAR OPENED
1989
DESIGN FIRM
Hunt Weber Clark Design
DESIGNER
Nancy Hunt-Weber
ILLUSTRATOR
Nancy Hunt-Weber
PRINTER
Fong & Fong

Postrio's menu had a San Francisco theme when the restaurant first opened in 1989. The management wanted to distance the restaurant from the location theme. ''They were looking to build on their well earned reputation for fresh and unusual food, great service and elegant dining,'' stated designer Nancy Hunt-Weber. Postrio's interior design was done by Pat Kuleto, and is intended to showcase the contemporary food. The decor features an eclectic collection of art and so an illustration style was chosen for the menu cover. A subtle connection between the interior space and the menu was accomplished by using a pattern that mimics the marble floor and carpet design.

Panorama

RESTAURANT/OPERATOR
Panorama—A Seasonal Cuisine
Restaurant
Calgary, Canada
YEAR OPENED
1960 opened, renovated 1990
DESIGN FIRM
Hoffmann & Angelic Design
DESIGNER
Andrea Hoffmann
ART DIRECTOR
Ivan Angelic
ILLUSTRATOR
Andrea Hoffmann
PRINTER
First Western Printing

Panorama is an elegant restaurant featuring seasonal cuisine. It has been in existence since the late 1960s and recently underwent a complete renovation. Revolving atop the Calgary Tower, it appeals to business executives and visitors alike. The panorama logo is evocative of the airy feeling one might experience while dining "among the clouds."

The menu, designed by Andrea Hoffmann, was intended to have an ethereal quality. Both the general manager and the marketing director of Calgary Tower were closely involved with Ms. Hoffmann in all aspects of the design process. It was printed on white paper stock and laminated for easy maintenance. The illustrations are soft pastels, inspired by the interior. Inside, a die-cut of mountains and clouds in each of the four corners creates a folder used to accommodate this seasonal menu.

Italia

RESTAURANT/OPERATOR
Italia
Seattle, WA
YEAR OPENED
1982
DESIGN FIRM
Hornall Anderson Design Works
DESIGNER
Julia LaPine
ART DIRECTOR
Jack Anderson
ILLUSTRATOR
Julia LaPine
PRINTER
Watermark Press

Located in a beautifully renovated building in Seattle, Italia is a contrast between traditional and contemporary styling. The challenge was to design a simple menu that could be easily updated to include the freshest in seasonal ingredients. The solution was to use two sheets of heavy gauge plastic with holes drilled at the bottom and top. Raffia ties were used to hold the laser printed insert sheet. The plastic material is contemporary and the hand tying lends a traditional touch to this sturdy presentation.

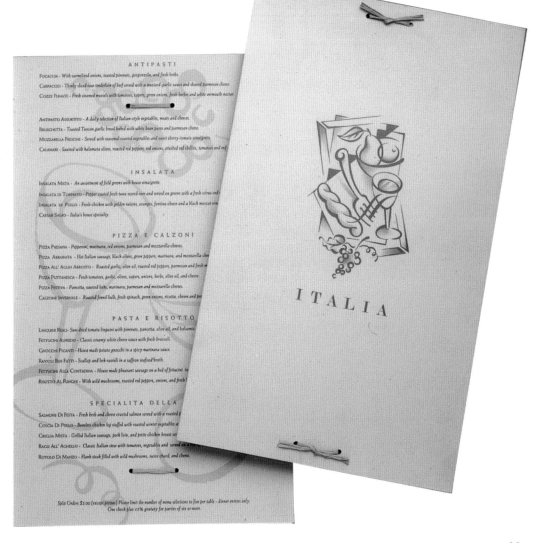

Chez Panisse

RESTAURANT/OPERATOR
Chez Panisse
Berkeley, CA
DESIGN FIRM
Patricia Curtan Design & Printing
DESIGNER
Patricia Curtan
ILLUSTRATOR
Patricia Curtan

Chez Panisse, noted for preparing a different menu each evening throughout the year, has a reputation for using the freshest available ingredients in novel ways. This unique dining experience requires a special menu presentation that is cost effective, and still as beautiful as the food it features. The menu covers, printed one at a time, are made from hand-cut linocut illustrations and printed on a letterpress. They were designed to be fed through a copier to accommodate the restaurant's need to make daily modifications. The covers are changed every two months to reflect the seasons.

Galeto's Restaurant

RESTAURANT/OPERATOR
Galeto's
New York, NY
DESIGN FIRM
Jennifer Clark Design
DESIGNER/ILLUSTRATOR
Jennifer Clark
PRINTER
DSS Printing

The restaurant wanted the menu to make a statement, hence this large scale, almost whimsical format was devised. Each of the entrees are handwritten in assorted colors and then laminated. The laminated surface allows the prices to be written in with magic marker. This provides the restaurant the opportunity to change pricing without having to reprint the menu. Overall, the style reflects a spirited approach to dining, as well as coordinating with the restaurant's color scheme.

Galeto's

Menu

Melon with Prosciutto
Gizzards with Bacon
Vegetable Soup
Cream of Asparagus

Cornish Hen
Turkey Breast Steak
Salmon Steak
Swordfish Steak
Filet Mignon
Rump Steak
New York Sirloin Steak
Pork Tenderloin
Half Filet Mignon / Half Pork Loin
(all entrées are charcoal broiled)

Mixed Salad
Garden Salad   Watercress Salad
Hearts of Palm Salad

Cheesecake
Chocolate Cake   Strawberry Cake
Creme Caramel   Melon
Chocolate Mousse   Ice Cream

Coffee   Decaf   Tea
Capuccino   Espresso

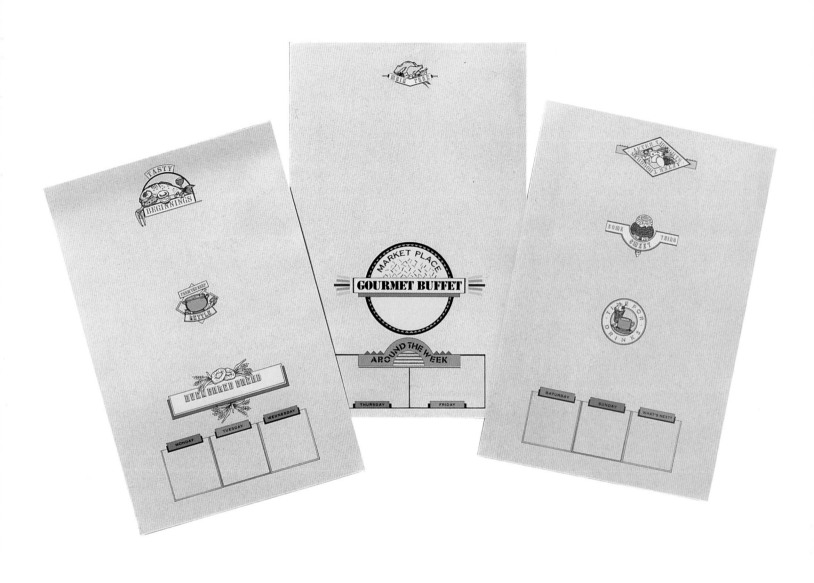

The Market Place Cafe

RESTAURANT/OPERATOR
Market Place Cafe
Adelaide Hilton International
Adelaide, Australia
YEAR OPENED
1982
DESIGN FIRM
in house
DESIGNER
Anna Sapio
ILLUSTRATOR
Anna Sapio
PRINTER
Finsbury Press

The Market Place Cafe in Adelaide, Australia, originally opened in 1982. They introduced this new format with its focus on earthy tones and bright lettering, in 1989. The designer, Anna Sapio, was trying to reflect an energetic new approach. A laminated placemat version is used for late suppers and busy lunches. The dinner menu is more formal and traditional, accommodating a laser printed insert produced via desktop publishing. The easy-to-read text was written by Jeanette Treffler.

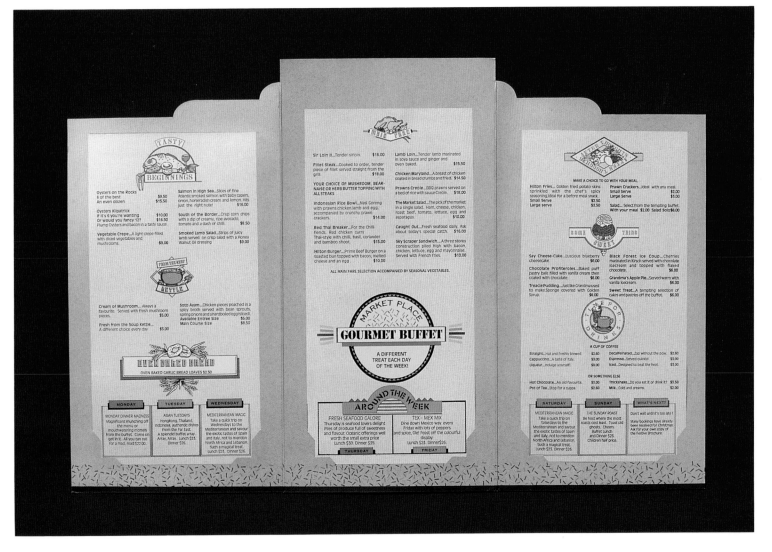

Restaurant Index

Designers Appendix

Great Menu Contest

The National Restaurant Association's annual Great Menu Contest offers foodservice operators a chance to earn recognition from their peers on the basis of their menus.

Menus are judged by a panel of food writers, editors and designers in nine categories: restaurant average check under $8 per person; restaurant average check $8–$15 per person; institutional foodservice; banquet/catering; specialty; most imaginative; best design and greatest merchandising power.

The judges score the entries on imagination, design and merchandising power. The winners of the Great Menu Contest receive a wooden plaque and menu stickers to display in their operations. These standard-setting menus are also displayed at the association's Restaurant, Hotel–Motel Show in Chicago and receive nationwide publicity. Many of the winners receive further exposure by their inclusion in this beautifully produced menu design book.

The Great Menu Contest is open to all foodservice operators. Designers are also welcome to enter, as long as the entry form is signed by the foodservice operator they represent. Contest entry forms are mailed in November and the deadline for entries is the end of February. 1993 will mark the Great Menu Contest's 30th anniversary of honoring the industry's finest menus.

For information about the contest, contact the National Restaurant Association, Communications Department, 1200 17th Street, N.W., Washington, D.C. 20036. Or call (202) 331-5900 or 1-800-424-5156.